W9-CHQ-692

# ENRICHING THE CHRISTIAN YEAR

# ENRICHING THE CHRISTIAN YEAR

compiled by
Michael Perham

with Trevor Lloyd, David Silk,
David Stancliffe and Michael Vasey

THE LITURGICAL PRESS
Collegeville, Minnesota

First published in Great Britain 1993
Society for Promoting Christian Knowledge
Holy Trinity Church
Marylebone Road
London NW1 4DU

Published in the United States of America
by the Liturgical Press, St John's Abbey,
Collegeville, Minnesota, 56321

Compilation © Michael Perham 1993. Copyright in individual items within the
book is retained by those named in Sources (pages 223–38).

All rights reserved. No part of this book may be reproduced or transmitted in
any form or by any means, electronic or mechanical, including photocopying,
recording, or by any information storage and retrieval system, without
permission in writing from the publisher.

ISBN 0–8146–2242–9

Printed in Great Britain

# CONTENTS

Acknowledgements     vi
Foreword *by Colin James, Bishop of Winchester*     vii
Introduction     ix
Guidelines     xiii

| | | |
|---|---|---|
| 1 | Lent | 1 |
| 2 | Mothering Sunday | 13 |
| 3 | Passiontide | 22 |
| 4 | Eastertide | 35 |
| 5 | Ascension | 48 |
| 6 | Pentecost | 58 |
| 7 | Trinity Sunday | 68 |
| 8 | The Transfiguration | 78 |
| 9 | Michaelmas | 85 |
| 10 | Dedication | 92 |

The Four Eucharistic Prayers from Rite A     100
Texts before the Distribution in Rite A     113

| | | |
|---|---|---|
| 11 | The Blessed Virgin Mary | 115 |
| 12 | Apostles and Evangelists | 125 |
| 13 | The Saints | 137 |
| 14 | Creation | 154 |
| 15 | Justice and Peace | 162 |
| 16 | Healing and Reconciliation | 174 |
| 17 | Baptism | 184 |
| 18 | The Word | 196 |
| 19 | Eucharist | 205 |
| 20 | Ministry | 214 |

Sources     223

# ACKNOWLEDGEMENTS

The compiler and the publishers are grateful to individuals, publishers and churches for their permission to reproduce copyright material in either original or adapted form.

Individual contributors listed in the Sources (see pages 223–38) retain copyright in their own material.

Material from the *Alternative Service Book 1980, Patterns for Worship, The Promise of His Glory*, and *Lent, Holy Week, Easter* is reproduced by permission of the copyright holder, the Central Board of Finance of the Church of England.

Thanks are also due to the following copyright holders:
The Anglican Church of Australia Trust Corporation, for material from *An Australian Prayer Book*, 1978.

The General Synod of the Anglican Church of Canada, for material from the Canadian *Book of Alternative Sources*, 1985.

The Church of the Province of New Zealand, for material from *A New Zealand Prayer Book – He Karakia Mihinare o Aotearoa*, 1989.

International Commission on English in the Liturgy, for excerpts from the English translation of *The Roman Missal*, © 1973.

The European Province of the Society of Saint Francis, for material from *The Daily Office SSF*, a prayer book for the use of the Society of Saint Francis; and *Celebrating Common Prayer: A Version of the Daily Office SSF*, published by Mowbray, a Cassell imprint, 1992.

GIA Publications Inc., Chicago, Illinois, for material from *Praise God in Song*.

Jubilate Hymns, for material from *Church Family Worship*, edited by Michael Perry, published by Hodder and Stoughton, 1986.

Charles MacDonnell, for material from *After Communion*, published by Mowbray, 1985.

Janet Morley, for material from *All Desires Known*, expanded edition published by SPCK, 1992.

David Silk, for material from *In Penitence and Faith: Texts for Use with the Alternative Services*, published by Mowbray, a Cassell imprint, 1988; and *Prayers for Use at the Alternative Services*, published by Mowbray, 1980.

Bryan Spinks, for material from *Christ Our Light*, published by Kevin Mayhew, 1980.

Biblical passages are reproduced with permission from The Revised Standard Version of the Bible (RSV), copyright 1946, 1952 © 1971, 1973 by The Division of Christian Education of the National Council of the Churches of Christ in the USA.

# FOREWORD

In the past twelve years following the authorization of the Alternative Service Book the Liturgical Commission has published a series of volumes for use in conjunction with it. The first to appear was *Lent, Holy Week, Easter* in 1986. It is noticeable that services provided in it are increasingly being used in our churches, and indeed now form a measure of common prayer which has hitherto been lacking at this season.

*The Promise of His Glory* (published in 1991) spans the period from All Saints' tide to Candlemas, 2 February. In some ways it complements *Lent, Holy Week, Easter* though the seasons and months it covers are more diverse in character than the forty days leading up to the Festival of Festivals. And the later book draws on a wider range of sources than its predecessors.

The remainder of the liturgical year is now being addressed by this third volume in the sequence, *Enriching the Christian Year*. Though it will be seen that there is also additional material for use in the earlier seasons, and on principal feast days, as well as in the period following Pentecost, specific themes such as Creation, and Justice and Peace, are provided for as well. The variety of material here, drawn from many sources yet also containing much fresh writing, can be used in the context of the Eucharist, or at Morning and Evening Prayer, as well as on other occasions. Yet the provision of texts, important as this is, is only one aspect in the offering of worship. It is the responsibility of the clergy to study and understand the liturgy, to give careful thought and teaching towards its preparation and presentation, so that God may be glorified and his people edified. Here, I hope that the guidelines will assist those who lead worship in the selection of material which is appropriate both to the particular season and occasion and also to the character and resources of the local church.

*Enriching the Christian Year* is not formally a publication of the Liturgical Commission, though its author and compilers are prominent members of that body. They have all been closely involved in the production of *The Promise of His Glory* and *Patterns for Worship*, which is proving to be a useful resource book in the worshipping life of many churches. Michael Perham, and those assisting him, have here produced an invaluable aid to deepen and develop the worship offered in our churches; and I pray that this book will fulfil the promise of its title and further enrich the Christian year. I wish to thank them, for the service they give to the Liturgical Commission, and not least for the friendship and forbearance they have extended to its chairman.

Wolvesey,                                        ✝ Colin Winton
Winchester                                  Bishop of Winchester
                            Chairman, The Liturgical Commission

May 1992

# INTRODUCTION

The authorization of *The Alternative Service Book 1980* opened up new possibilities for worship in the Church of England. Like nearly all opportunities for change, they were fraught with danger. There was now new permission for the leader of worship, whether president at the eucharist, or other ministers in a number of other settings, to use his or her own words, or to introduce other material, old or new, from other sources. 'These or other suitable words' has been a common rubric in modern Anglican liturgy.

Not everyone has rushed to use the new permissions. Sometimes this has been wise, representing a desire not to lose well-tried and well-loved texts, some of them modified only a little from their Book of Common Prayer originals. Or sometimes it has been a reluctance to introduce so much variety into worship that there is no sense of either continuity from one service to another or of common prayer shared among many churches.

Nevertheless in many communities a great diversity of texts has come into use. Some of this has been creative and enriching. Some of it has been poor, whether the poverty has been in the language, or in the theology, or in the liturgical appropriateness.

This book is intended to help those who lead worship to be able to draw on a rich resource at all the points where there is freedom to find the best text for a particular occasion or a particular community. But it is not the first book in the field. Indeed what it is really trying to do is to plug a gap, that otherwise might remain until the year 2000, after the publication in recent years of three books from the Church of England's Liturgical Commission.

The first of these was *Lent, Holy Week, Easter*, commended by the House of Bishops for use from 1986. *Lent, Holy Week, Easter* provided full service forms for the great days leading up to and including Easter Day, but it was also a resource book that enabled people to find good material, Anglican in character, for use in many different services through Lent and Eastertide.

It was not surprising that there was soon demand for something equivalent for the other great cycle of the Christian year, through Advent to Christmas and on to Epiphany. This was published as *The Promise of His Glory* and commended by the House of Bishops in 1991. The Commission broadened the book's reference to begin with All Saintstide and to end with the Feast of the Presentation, Candlemas.

People joked that what was needed now was a third volume called 'Pentecost to Michaelmas', and to some extent that is what this book tries to be. But in fact the picture is more complex. For *The Promise of His Glory* made, for the three months it covers, far richer provision than the earlier *Lent, Holy Week, Easter* made for its three months. So, for instance, those who use *The Promise* become used to the provision of a Solemn Blessing for great festivals like Christmas and Epiphany, but then find there are none for Easter and Ascension. Or they come to appreciate the Service for the Blessing of Light on Saturday evening through Advent, Christmas and Epiphany, but then find they have no texts for its use in Lent or Eastertide. So, in addition to plugging the gaps by providing for the festivals and seasons that the other two books did not tackle, *Enriching the Christian Year* has also tried to 'top up' the Lent and Eastertide material to the level that *The Promise* provides before and after Christmas.

In the cycle of the seasons, material has therefore been given for Lent, Passiontide, Easter, Ascension and Pentecost. Provision has not been made for Advent, Christmas and Epiphany simply because they are thoroughly treated in *The Promise of His Glory*.

Additionally we have provided for other holy days and commemorations in the Christian year – Mothering Sunday, Trinity Sunday, the Transfiguration, Michaelmas, the Feast of Dedication, and the festivals of apostles and evangelists, martyrs and other saints. There is no material for All Saints' Day, the Commemoration of the Faithful Departed, Remembrance Day or Candlemas, because *The Promise* does this fully.

The seven final chapters cover major Christian themes that may occur at different times of the year. These are 'Creation' (which includes Rogationtide and Harvest), 'Justice and Peace', 'Healing and Reconciliation', 'Baptism', 'The Word', 'Eucharist' and 'Ministry'.

Two other areas of equal importance that we have chosen not to cover, are 'Christian Unity' and 'Mission and Evangelism', again simply because *The Promise* does this so fully in its Epiphany material.

The third book from the Liturgical Commission has been *Patterns for Worship*, published in 1989. This resource book, which is now undergoing revision before reissue, has broken new ground in liturgical provision, and we have drawn widely on it.

*Enriching the Christian Year* includes material from all three books, as well as from the ASB, where it sometimes brings into prominence appendix material sometimes neglected, and other recent service books. We have also gone to the Book of Common Prayer and the 1928 Book, conscious that the fashion for novelty in the 1970s and 1980s has allowed some fine prayers to be lost. Nevertheless much of the provision here is newly written, and tries to respond to the contemporary mood for a more poetic and rhythmic approach to writing liturgy than the sometimes terse style of the ASB. Wherever we have drawn on the material of other Churches, including the Roman Missal, we have amended and adapted to enable the material to fit our Anglican worship, and both in amending older material and also in composing new we have tried to be sensitive to the issue of inclusive language and to affirm the feminine.

Each of the twenty chapters is divided into three parts. The first part includes texts that could be employed at any service. The second part has material specifically for the eucharist. The third part makes provision for Morning and Evening Prayer, though some of this might have a wider application.

MICHAEL PERHAM

# GUIDELINES

## Invitation to Confession

These texts, most of which are quotations or adaptations from Scripture, are for use to introduce the prayers of penitence at any service. At the eucharist, ASB Rite A specifically mentions 'other suitable words at this point'. They would normally be followed by a time of silence before the confession.

## Penitential Kyrie

Although the *Kyrie* was not originally a penitential text in the eucharist, it has found a usefulness in contemporary liturgy either as an alternative to the more festal *Gloria* or as a short and responsorial form of confession. The forms provided here, with a sentence (very often, though not invariably, of Scripture) in each of the three sections are for this penitential use, where invitation would be followed by short silence, the *Kyrie* in this form, and then a brief absolution. A simple form of absolution is

> May almighty God have mercy on us,
> forgive us our sins,
> and bring us to everlasting life. **Amen.**

Although the *Kyrie* has associations with the eucharist, these forms could be used at other services also.

The invariable use of this style of confession, to the exclusion of a full text of the sort given in Holy Communion Rite A or Morning and Evening Prayer, would not do justice to the place that corporate penitence has in Anglican worship.

## Intercession

These Intercessions, suitable for the eucharist and for other services, are, in the main, intended for use with the insertion of local material, introducing particular prayer intentions. In some cases the shape and style of the prayer would make interpolation difficult, and here it is recommended that any local material should precede the prayer in the form of biddings. Even when the printed text and the local insertions are intermingled, care should be taken to respect the style of the prayer and not to imbalance its sentences with overmuch additional material.

The majority of the sets of Intercessions here conform to the ASB norm of five sections (Church, World, Local Community, Those who Suffer, The Departed), but not all do so, and careful preparation is therefore important where local intentions are to be inserted.

Where an unfamiliar congregational response is to be used, the leader needs to give this clearly at the beginning. It is always best, having given the response, to use it *immediately*. This helps the congregation to assimilate it.

Silence is nearly always an important element in intercession if the people are to have the opportunity to pray and to make the intentions their own.

When an Intercession ends with a concluding collect, this may be said by the same person who has led the whole Intercession, but it may also be appropriately said by the minister who presides at the service.

## *Acclamation*

These acclamations, nearly all of them scriptural, may be used in a variety of contexts. Sometimes they might give a seasonal flavour to the service at the very beginning before the opening hymn or after the Greeting. They might also be used before, between or after readings. At a Word Service they could well be part of a climax at the end. A repeated two-line acclamation can be used repeatedly through a service, both to call people back to a theme, and also to mark the transition from one stage of the service to the next.

## Simple Blessing

These add to the collection in ASB Rite A. In some cases they are additional to ASB provision. In others they provide for a season, festival or theme for which the ASB has no text. Many of them can be adapted simply for a service ending by a lay person.

## Solemn Blessing

*Patterns for Worship* and *The Promise of His Glory* introduced Solemn Blessings into Church of England practice. They are a feature of modern Roman Catholic liturgy, though those in *Patterns* and *The Promise* and those in this book are different in style, following in the main a more trinitarian shape, whereby each of the first three clauses refers to one person of the Trinity, and the three are brought together in the usual trinitarian formula of the final clause. They mark out a particular day or service as special, and they bring back right at the end of the liturgy some of the major themes it will have celebrated.

## Introduction to the Peace

Experience has shown that the over-use of the didactic 'We are the Body of Christ . . .' text is unhelpful, and this is one of the points where a variety of texts is refreshing. The texts here are almost all scriptural and focus on Christian peace and reconciliation.

Although these are given as eucharistic texts, they are, of course, appropriate where the Greeting of Peace has been incorporated into other services.

## Eucharistic Preface

The provision of proper prefaces in ASB Rite A is very uneven. For some seasons such as Christmas and Easter there is a variety of good material. At other times it is very thin. These prefaces draw in other material, including Prayer Book and Rite B material. Some of them are longer than the ASB prefaces, and would best be used with a shorter lead in, such as Eucharistic Prayer 2 indicates.

## Words at the Breaking of Bread
## Invitation to Communion

Because these are texts involving congregational response, they cannot be used unless the congregation has the words printed in front of them, unless by consistent use throughout a season a particular text becomes sufficiently familiar for use without. Because this is unlikely to be a good moment in the service for the unfamiliar, only a limited number of texts has been given here, and of course not all of these need be used.

Although a seasonal element here will sometimes be beneficial, the necessary blend of familiar and variable could mean that a special text were used for the Breaking of Bread *or* the Invitation to Communion, but not both.

## Prayers after Communion

ASB Rite A allows a variable prayer after communion, and such a prayer, bringing back a seasonal element, is often the right conclusion to a time of silent prayer after the distribution. This prayer may be alternative to, or additional to, a prayer, such as Rite A's 'Almighty God, we thank you for feeding us . . .', said by the congregation together.

Some, but not all, of the prayers in this collection are themselves suitable as congregational prayers. Some, but not all, are also suitable at the end of non-eucharistic services.

# Light Prayer

*The Promise of His Glory* provides a Service of Light for use at dusk, at the beginning of Evening Prayer, a vigil service, or other forms of worship at the end of the day, but its seasonal provision of prayers to acclaim the light is restricted to the Advent to Candlemas period. The provision here covers the rest of the year. The Light Blessing is traditionally part of the deacon's liturgical ministry. Its style invites it to be sung.

# Canticles

A wealth of canticles, most of them based on Scripture, is becoming available in the Church today, and those provided here are not intended to discourage the use of others. But for those who, until now, have been content with the ASB canticles, here are two for each season, festival and theme. They are given as part of the provision for Daily Prayer, but they could be used between readings at the eucharist, or included in other services.

They have been provided with a congregational response, and an indication of the points at which to use that response, but equally they can be used in other ways and the response simply omitted.

# Patterns of Readings with Psalms and Canticles

This section extends to the whole year provision that *The Promise of His Glory* made for the Advent to Candlemas period. The sets of readings, most of them consisting of five Old Testament passages with an Epistle and finally a Gospel, are a resource for use in different ways, though with a night vigil service as a norm. The lections can be used with the psalms and canticles, or other musical provision can be made between the lections.

## *Ending*

These are concluding words for any service. Most of them do not
have the blessing shape found earlier in each section. Some of them
involve congregational response, but most could be used by the
minister alone.

# 1 LENT

## Invitation to Confession

1    The sacrifice of God is a broken spirit;
a broken and contrite heart he will not despise.
Our sin is always before us:
we acknowledge our transgressions in penitence and faith.   *1 A 1*

2    Compassion and forgiveness belong to the Lord our God,
though we have rebelled against him.
Let us then renounce our wilfulness and ask his mercy
by confessing our sins in penitence and faith.   *1 A 2*

## Penitential Kyrie

Wash me thoroughly from my wickedness
and cleanse me from my sin:
Lord, have mercy.
**Lord, have mercy.**

Create in me a clean heart, O God,
and renew a right spirit within me:
Christ, have mercy.
**Christ, have mercy.**

Cast me not away from your presence,
and take not your Holy Spirit from me.
Lord, have mercy.
**Lord, have mercy.**   *1 B 1*

## Intercession

1    With confidence and trust let us pray to the Father, saying
Lord of compassion,
**in your mercy hear us.**

For the one holy catholic and apostolic Church . . .
let us pray to the Father.

Lord of compassion,
**in your mercy hear us.**

For the mission of the Church,
that in faithful witness it may preach the gospel
   to the ends of the earth,
let us pray to the Father.

Lord of compassion,
**in your mercy hear us.**

For those preparing for baptism (and confirmation) . . .
and for their teachers and sponsors,
let us pray to the Father.

Lord of compassion,
**in your mercy hear us.**

For peace in the world . . .
that a spirit of respect and reconciliation may grow
   among nations and peoples,
let us pray to the Father.

Lord of compassion,
**in your mercy hear us.**

For the poor, the persecuted, the sick, and all who suffer . . . ;
for refugees, prisoners, and all in danger;
that they may be relieved and protected,
let us pray to the Father.

Lord of compassion,
**in your mercy hear us.**

For those whom we have injured or offended,
let us pray to the Father.

Lord of compassion,
**in your mercy hear us.**

For grace to amend our lives and to further the reign of God,
let us pray to the Father.

Lord of compassion,
**in your mercy hear us.**

In communion with all those who have walked in the way of
   holiness . . .
let us pray to the Father.

Lord of compassion,
**in your mercy hear us.**

God our Father,
in your love and goodness
you have taught us to come close to you in penitence
with prayer, fasting and generosity;
accept our Lenten discipline,
and when we fall by our weakness,
raise us up by your unfailing mercy;
through Jesus Christ our Lord.   **Amen.**                    *1 C 1*

2    We pray to the Lord for courage to give up other things
     and to give ourselves to him this Lent, saying

Lord, meet us in the silence,
**give us strength and hear our prayer.**

Give your Church the courage
to give up her preoccupation with herself
and to give more time to your mission in the world.
(We pray for N our bishop and . . . )

May the blood and water flowing from the side of Jesus
bring forgiveness to your people
and help us to face the cost of proclaiming salvation.

Lord, meet us in the silence,
**give us strength and hear our prayer.**

Give your world the courage
to give up war, bitterness and hatred,
and to seek peace.
(We pray for . . .)

May the shoulders of the risen Jesus, once scourged by soldiers,
bear the burden of political and military conflict in our world.

Lord, meet us in the silence,
**give us strength and hear our prayer.**

Give us the courage to give up quarrels, strife and jealousy
in our families, neighbourhoods and communities.
(We pray for . . .)

May the presence of the risen Jesus,
his body once broken and now made whole,
bring peace and direction as we live with one another.

Lord, meet us in the silence,
**give us strength and hear our prayer.**

Give us the courage
to give up our selfishness as we live for others,
and to give time, care and comfort to the sick.
(We pray for . . .)

May the wounded hands of Jesus bring his healing touch,
and the light of his presence fill their rooms.

Lord, meet us in the silence,
**give us strength and hear our prayer.**

Give us the courage to give up our fear of death
and to rejoice with those who have died in faith.
(Especially we hold . . . in our minds.)

May the feet of the risen Lord Jesus, once nailed to the cross,
walk alongside the dying and bereaved in their agony,
and walk with us and all your Church
through death to the gate of glory.

Lord, meet us in the silence,
**give us strength and hear our prayer,**
**here and in eternity.   Amen.**                          *1 C 2*

## Acclamation

Save your people, Lord, and bless your inheritance:
**govern and uphold them now and always.**
Day by day we bless you:
**we praise your name for ever.**
Keep us today (tonight), Lord, from all sin:
**have mercy on us, Lord, have mercy.**
Lord show us your love and mercy:
**for we put our trust in you.**
In you Lord is our hope:
**let us not be confounded at the last.**                  *1 D 1*

## Simple Blessing

1    Christ give you grace to grow in holiness,
     to deny yourselves,
     take up your cross,
     and follow him;
     and the blessing . . .                                *1 E 1*

2    God,
     who from the death of sin raised you to new life in Christ,
     keep you from falling and set you in the presence of his glory;
     and the blessing . . .                                *1 E 2*

5

## Solemn Blessing for Ash Wednesday

May God the Father,
who does not despise the broken spirit,
give to you a contrite heart.  **Amen.**

May Christ,
who bore our sins in his body on the tree,
heal you by his wounds.  **Amen.**

May the Holy Spirit,
who leads us into all truth,
speak to you words of pardon and peace.  **Amen.**

And the blessing . . .                                      1 F 1


## THE EUCHARIST

## Introduction to the Peace

Being justified by faith,
we have peace with God through our Lord Jesus Christ.   1 G 1


## Eucharistic Preface

1    And now we give you thanks
     because through him you have given us the spirit of discipline,
     that we may triumph over evil and grow in grace.
     Therefore . . .                                      1 H 1

2    And now we give you thanks
     because he was tempted in every way as we are,
     yet did not sin.
     By his grace we are able to triumph over every evil,
     and to live no longer for ourselves alone,
     but for him who died for us and rose again.
     Therefore . . .                                      1 H 2

3    And now we give you thanks
because each year you give us this joyful season
when we prepare to celebrate the paschal mystery
with mind and heart renewed.
You give us a spirit of loving reverence for you
and of willing service to our neighbour.
As we recall the saving acts that give new life in Christ,
you bring the image of your Son to perfection
    within our hearts.
Therefore . . .                     *1 H 3*

## *Words at the Breaking of Bread*

Every time we eat this bread
and drink this cup:
**we proclaim the Lord's death
until he comes.**                  *1 J 1*

## *Invitation to Communion*

Jesus is the Lamb of God who takes away the sins of the world.
Happy are those who are called to his supper.
**Lord, I am not worthy to receive you,
but only say the word and I shall be healed.**    *1 K 1*

## *Prayers after Communion*

1    God of compassion,
through your Son Jesus Christ
you have reconciled your people to yourself.
As we follow his example of prayer and fasting,
may we obey you with willing hearts
and serve one another in holy love;
through Jesus Christ our Lord.  **Amen.**     *1 L 1*

2    Eternal God,
    comfort of the afflicted and healer of the broken,
    you have fed us at the table of life and hope.
    Teach us the ways of gentleness and peace,
    that all the world may acknowledge
    the kingdom of your Son Jesus Christ our Lord.  **Amen.**   *1 L 2*

3    God of our pilgrimage,
    you have led us to the living water.
    Refresh and sustain us
    as we go forward on our journey,
    in the name of Jesus Christ our Lord.  **Amen.**   *1 L 3*

From Lent 1 onwards the collect of Ash Wednesday is suitable as a prayer after Communion.

DAILY PRAYER

*Light Prayer*

    Blessed are you, O Lord our God.
    the shepherd of Israel,
    their pillar of cloud by day,
    their pillar of fire by night.
    In these forty days you lead us
    into the desert of repentance
    that in this pilgrimage of prayer
    we may learn to be your people once more.
    In fasting and service
    you bring us back to your heart.
    You open our eyes to your presence in the world
    and you free our hands to lead others
    to the radiant splendour of your mercy.
    Be with us in these journey days
    for without you we are lost and will perish.
    To you alone be dominion and glory,
    for ever and ever.  **Amen.**   *1 M 1*

# Canticles

1 A SONG OF HOSEA

[Response **Come let us return to the Lord.**]

1 Come, let us return to the Lord:
who has torn us and will heal us.

2 God has stricken us:
and will bind up our wounds.

3 After two days, God will revive us:
and on the third day will raise us up,
that we may live in the presence of God. **[R]**

4 Let us humble ourselves,
let us strive to know our God:
whose justice dawns like the morning star
and its dawning is as sure as the sunrise.

5 God's justice will come to us like the showers:
like the spring rains that water the earth. **[R]**

6 O Ephraim, how shall I deal with you?:
How shall I deal with you, O Judah?

7 Your love for me is like the morning mist:
like the dew that goes early away. **[R]**

8 Therefore I have hewn them by the prophets:
and my judgement goes forth as the light.

9 For loyalty is my desire and not sacrifice:
and the knowledge of God rather than burnt-offerings. **[R]** *1 N 1*

## 2 A SONG OF REPENTANCE (A SONG OF ISAIAH)

[Response **Let us return to the Lord**
**who will richly pardon.**]

1    Seek the Lord while he may be found:
     call upon him while he is near.

2    Let the wicked forsake their ways:
     and the unrighteous their thoughts.

3    Let them return to the Lord,
     who will have mercy on them:
     and to our God, who will richly pardon.   **[R]**

4    For my thoughts are not your thoughts, says the Lord:
     neither are your ways my ways.

5    As the heavens are higher than the earth:
     so are my ways higher than your ways,
     and my thoughts than your thoughts.   **[R]**

6    And as the rain and snow come down from heaven:
     and return not again but water the earth,

7    Bringing forth life and giving growth:
     seed for sowing and bread for eating,

8    So shall the word which comes forth from my mouth prevail:
     and succeed in the task I give it.   **[R]**                    1 N 2


# Patterns of Readings with Psalms and Canticles

# 1   Theme: Penitence

*suitable also for Shrove Tuesday*

1    Joshua 24.1–2a, 14–27
     Psalm 102.1–11, 19–end

2   Hosea 14.1–7
      Psalm 38

3   Amos 5.6–13
      Psalm 6

4   Isaiah 58.1–8
      Psalm 32

5   Ezekiel 18.21–end
      Psalm 51.1–17

6   1 Corinthians 9.24–end
      Psalm 143.1–11

Gospel   Luke 18.9–14

> If Psalm 130 is used later in the service all Penitential Psalms
> will have been used.                                           *1 P 1*

## 2 *Theme: A Lenten Sequence from St John's Gospel*

1   John 2.1–11
      Psalm 135.1–6, 21

2   John 4.46–end
      Psalm 30.1–3, 11–12

3   John 5.1–15
      Psalm 40.1–7

4   John 6.4–15
      Psalm 147.12–end

5   John 9.1–13, 28–38
      Psalm 36.5–10

6   John 11.18–44
      A Song of Redemption (*The Promise* page 328)

Gospel   John 20.1–9(10–18)                                      *1 P 2*

## *Ending*

Joy with peace,
amendment of life,
time for true repentance,
the grace and comfort of the Holy Spirit,
and perseverance in good works,
grant us, O almighty and merciful Lord.   **Amen.**   *1 Q 1*

# 2  MOTHERING SUNDAY

The Fourth Sunday in Lent is very widely observed as Mothering Sunday. It is difficult to combine this observance with the ASB material for Lent 4 with its Transfiguration theme, and, even without that theme, there is the difficulty of finding a way of observing Mothering Sunday in such a way that it does not cut right across the feel of Lent.

Nevertheless, pastorally Mothering Sunday is full of potential, and it will nearly always be unwise to ignore this. It is possible to keep something of the Lenten flavour if the suffering of Mary is used as the theme that holds together the concerns of Mothering Sunday and the development of Lent as it moves towards the passion. John 19.25–27 is the obvious lection (and Gospel for the eucharist), though Luke 2.33–35 could also serve, and Exodus 2.1–10, 2 Corinthians 1.3–7 and Colossians 3.12–17 are also suitable.

## *A Collect*

God of compassion,
whose Son Jesus Christ, the child of Mary,
shared the life of a home in Nazareth,
and on the cross drew the whole human family to himself:
strengthen us in our daily living
that in our joys and in our sorrows
we may know your presence to bind together and to heal;
through Jesus Christ our Lord,
who is alive and reigns with you and the Holy Spirit,
one God, now and for ever.  **Amen.**                    *2 X 1*

Or the collect of the Annunciation or of Christmas 2 (Year 1), though this latter does not retain any of the Lent/Approaching Passion element.

## Invitation to Confession

1    Jesus said,
Before you offer your gift, go and be reconciled.
As brothers and sisters in God's family,
we come together to ask his forgiveness.    *2 A 1*

2    We have done what was wrong in the Lord's sight
and chosen what displeased him.
Yet as a mother comforts her child,
so shall the Lord himself comfort us.
So let us come to him who knows our every deed and thought.

    *2 A 2*

## Penitential Kyrie

As a father is tender towards his children,
so is the Lord tender to those that fear him:
Lord, have mercy.
**Lord, have mercy.**

He will not always be chiding,
nor will he keep his anger for ever:
Christ, have mercy.
**Christ, have mercy.**

I have calmed and quieted my soul,
like a child upon its mother's breast is my soul within me:
Lord, have mercy.
**Lord, have mercy.**    *2 B 1*

## Intercession

1    We pray for the family of the Church and for the life of families
around us, saying
Father of all
**hear your children's prayer.**

Sovereign Lord, your Son has revealed you as our heavenly Father, from whom every family in heaven and on earth is named . . .
Father of all
**hear your children's prayer.**

You have made your Church a spiritual family, a household of faith. Through baptism we are reborn as the brothers and sisters of Christ. Deepen our unity and fellowship in him . . .
Father of all
**hear your children's prayer.**

You sent your Son to give his life as a ransom for the whole human family. Give justice, peace and racial harmony to the world he died to save . . .
Father of all
**hear your children's prayer.**

You gave your Son a share in the life of a family in Nazareth. Help us to value our families, to be thankful for them, and to live sensitively within them . . .
Father of all
**hear your children's prayer.**

Your Son drew around him a company of friends. Bring love and joy to all who are alone. Help us all to find in the brothers and sisters of Christ a loving family . . .
Father of all
**hear your children's prayer.**

You are the God of the dead as well as of the living. In confidence we remember those of the household of faith who have gone before us . . . Bring us with them to the joy of your home in heaven, where you are alive and reign now and for ever. **Amen.**                                    *2 C 1*

2     For all our mothers and fathers,
      **Lord, receive our thanks and prayer.**

For the security of homes and family life,
**Lord, receive our thanks and prayer.**

For the joy of all loving human relationships,
**Lord, receive our thanks and prayer.**

For your holy catholic Church, the mother of us all,
**Lord, receive our thanks and prayer.**

For your family in this place, and our life together,
**Lord, receive our thanks and prayer.**

For all the members of our families who have died,
and now find their home in you,
**Lord, receive our thanks and prayer.**

For Mary, the Mother of Jesus,
and for all who seek to follow her example of motherhood,
**Lord, receive our thanks and prayer.**                2 C 2


## Acclamation

Blessed is everyone who fears the Lord:
and walks in the confines of his ways.
**Come, my children, listen to me:**
**and I will teach you the fear of the Lord.**
You will eat the fruit of your labours:
happy shall you be and all shall go well with you.
**Come, my children, listen to me:**
**and I will teach you the fear of the Lord.**
Unless the Lord builds the house:
their labour is but lost that build it.
**Come, my children, listen to me:**
**and I will teach you the fear of the Lord.**
Unless the Lord keeps the city:
the watchmen watch in vain.
**Come, my children, listen to me:**
**and I will teach you the fear of the Lord.**                2 D 1

## Simple Blessing

May the Father from whom every family
in earth and heaven receives its name
strengthen you with his Spirit in your inner being
so that Christ may dwell in your hearts by faith
(and that, knowing his love,
broad and long, deep and high beyond all knowledge,
you may be filled with all the fulness of God);
and the blessing . . .                                  *2 E 1*

## Solemn Blessing

When the Word became flesh
earth was joined to heaven in the womb of Mary:
may the love and obedience of Mary
be your example. **Amen.**

May the peace of Christ
rule in your hearts and homes. **Amen.**

May you be filled with the joys of the Spirit
and the gifts of your eternal home. **Amen.**

And the blessing . . .                                  *2 F 1*

THE EUCHARIST

It is important to maintain the Lent feel to the day through some of
the material at the eucharist. What follows is not therefore full
provision for the eucharist, but see instead the previous chapter.

## Introduction to the Peace

> Jesus said,
> 'Whoever does the will of God
> is my brother, and sister and mother.'
> As we have opportunity, let us work for good to all,
> especially to members of the household of faith.   *2 G 1*

## Eucharistic Preface

1   And now we give you thanks
    because your eternal Word took our nature upon him
    in the womb of Mary the Virgin.
    The sword of sorrow pierced her heart
    when he was lifted high on the cross,
    and by his sacrifice made our peace with you.
    Therefore . . .   *2 H 1*

2   And now we give you thanks
    because in his earthly childhood
    you entrusted him to the care of a human family.
    In Mary and Joseph you give us
       an example of love and devotion to him,
    and also a pattern of family life.
    Therefore . . .   *2 H 2*

## Prayers after Communion

1   Father of all, you gathered us here
    around the table of your Son;
    we have shared this meal with saints
    and the whole fellowship of the household of God.
    In that new world
    where the fulness of your peace will be revealed,
    gather people of every race, language and way of life
    to share in the one eternal banquet
    of Jesus Christ the Lord.   **Amen.**   *2 L 1*

2   Loving God,
    as a mother feeds her children at the breast
    you feed us in this sacrament
        with the food and drink of eternal life:
    help us who have tasted your goodness
    to grow in grace within the household of faith;
    through Jesus Christ our Lord.   **Amen.**                    *2 L 2*

## DAILY PRAYER

## *Light Prayer*

Blessed are you, Sovereign God, gentle and merciful:
to you be glory and praise for ever!
Your Spirit breathed over the chaos;
and now renews the face of the earth.
When we turned to darkness and chaos,
like a mother you would not forsake us.
You cried out like a woman in labour
and rejoiced to bring forth a new people.
In Christ you delivered us from darkness
to the gentle rule of your love.
**Blessed be God for ever!**                                    *2 M 1*

## *Canticle*

### THE SONG OF ANSELM

[Response   Either **Jesus, as a mother you gather your people to
              you.**
         or   **In your love and tenderness remake us.**]

1   Jesus, as a mother you gather your people to you:
    you are gentle with us as a mother with her children;

2   Often you weep over our sins and our pride:
    tenderly you draw us from hatred and judgement.   **[R]**

19

3    You comfort us in sorrow and bind up our wounds:
     in sickness you nurse us, and with pure milk you feed us.

4    Jesus, by your dying we are born to new life:
     by your anguish and labour we come forth in joy.   **[R]**

5    Despair turns to hope through your sweet goodness:
     through your gentleness we find comfort in fear.

6    Your warmth gives life to the dead:
     your touch makes sinners righteous.   **[R]**

7    Lord Jesus, in your mercy heal us:
     in your love and tenderness remake us.

8    In your compassion bring grace and forgiveness:
     for the beauty of heaven may your love prepare us.   **[R]**    *2 N 1*


## Pattern of Readings with Psalms and Canticles

1    Genesis 1.26–28,31a or
     Genesis 2.4–9,15–24
         Psalm 121

2    Genesis 23.1–4,19; 24.1–8,62–end
         Psalm 128

3    1 Samuel 1.20–end
         Canticle: Song of Hannah (see Chapter 11)
or
     Ruth 1.8–17,22
         Psalm 122

4    Proverbs 31.10–end
         Psalm 127

5    2 Timothy 1.3–10
         Psalm 37.3–6
or

Tobit 8.5b–8
Canticle: Song of Tobit (*The Promise* page 318)

6    Ephesians 5.26—6.4
Canticle: A Song of God's Grace (*The Promise* page 329) or
Canticle: A Song of the Holy City (*The Promise* page 332)

Gospel   Matthew 7.21,24–27 or
John 19.23–29                                    *2 P 1*

# *Ending*

May we obey like Mary and work hard like Joseph,
and may the childlike joy and devotion and love of Jesus
be with us as we continue to grow
in the grace and knowledge of our Lord and Saviour,
to whom be glory now and for all eternity.  **Amen.**   *2 Q 1*

# 3  PASSIONTIDE

No modern calendar (nor indeed the calendar of the Book of Common Prayer) designates the Fifth Sunday in Lent 'Passion Sunday', and this for the very good reason that Palm Sunday, the first day of Holy Week, is essentially the Sunday of the Passion. Nevertheless there is good reason for a change of gear on Lent 5, and for the introduction of material that paves the way for Holy Week.

The material in this chapter is therefore suitable for the last two weeks before Easter, though it is simply a supplement to the rich provision in *Lent, Holy Week, Easter*. It is also suitable for other occasions in the year that focus on the cross and the passion, particularly for Holy Cross Day on 14 September.


## Invitation to Confession

1    Christ himself bore our sins in his body on the tree,
     that we might die to sin and live to righteousness.
     By his wounds we are healed.
     Let us confess our sins.                                    *3 A 1*

2    God shows his love for us
     in that while we were still sinners Christ died for us.
     Let us then show our love for him
     by confessing our sins in penitence and faith.              *3 A 2*


## Penitential Kyrie

    Lord Jesus,
    you came to reconcile us to one another and the Father:
    Lord, have mercy.
    **Lord, have mercy.**

Lord Jesus,
you heal the wounds of sin and division:
Christ, have mercy.
**Christ, have mercy.**

Lord Jesus,
you intercede for us with your Father:
Lord, have mercy.
**Lord, have mercy.**                              *3 B 1*

## *Intercession*

1    Let us pray to the Father through his Son
who suffered on the cross for the world's redemption, and say
By the Saviour's cross and passion,
**Lord, save us and help us.**

Fill with your Spirit Christ's broken body, the Church . . .
Give to Christian people everywhere a deep longing
to take up the cross and to understand its mysterious glory.

By the Saviour's cross and passion,
**Lord, save us and help us.**

Bless those who lead the Church's worship at this solemn time
   . . .
In the preaching of the word
   and the celebration of the sacraments
draw your people close to you.

By the Saviour's cross and passion,
**Lord, save us and help us.**

Strengthen those (among us) who are preparing for baptism,
together with their teachers, sponsors and families . . .
Teach them what it means to die and rise with Christ
and prepare them to receive the breath of his Spirit.

By the Saviour's cross and passion,
**Lord, save us and help us.**

Look in your mercy upon the world you loved so much
that you sent your Son to suffer and to die . . .
Strengthen those who work to share
the reconciliation won at such a cost upon the cross.

By the Saviour's cross and passion,
**Lord, save us and help us.**

Bring healing by the wounds of Christ
to all who are weighed down by pain and injustice . . .
Help the lonely and the betrayed, the suffering and the dying,
to find strength in the companionship of Jesus,
and in his passion to know their salvation.

By the Saviour's cross and passion,
**Lord, save us and help us.**

Welcome into paradise all who have left this world in your
    friendship . . .
According to your promises,
bring them with all your saints to share
in all the benefits of Christ's death and resurrection.

By the Saviour's cross and passion,
**Lord, save us and help us.**

**[Holy God, holy and strong,**
**holy and immortal,**
**have mercy on us.]**                                    3 C 1

2    Let us pray to the Father,
     who loved the world so much that he sent his only Son
     to give us life.

     Simon from Cyrene was forced to carry the cross for your Son.
     Give us grace to lift heavy loads off those we meet
     and to put ourselves with those condemned to die.

     Lord, hear us.
     **Lord, graciously hear us.**

Your Son watched the soldiers gamble to share his clothes.
Look with your forgiveness
   on those who make a profit from their victims,
   and on those whose hearts may be hardened by their work.

Lord, hear us.
**Lord, graciously hear us.**

The thief looked for a part in the coming of your kingdom,
and received your Son's words of hope and comfort.
Give hope and reconciliation, healing and peace
   to all who look death in the face today.

Lord, hear us.
**Lord, graciously hear us.**

In Mary and John your Son created a new family at the cross.
Fill our relationships, and those of new families today,
   with mutual care and responsibility,
and give us a secure hope for the future.

Lord, hear us.
**Lord, graciously hear us.**

The centurion was astonished to see your glory
   in the crucified Messiah.
Open the eyes of those who are not yet your people
   to see in your Son the meaning of life and death.

Lord, hear us.
**Lord, graciously hear us.**

Nicodemus came to take your Son's body away.
Give gentleness, hope and faith
   to all who minister to the dying and bereaved,
   and courage to those whose faith is secret.

Lord, hear us.
**Lord, graciously hear us.**

Simon and Nicodemus, Mary and John
became part of your Church in Jerusalem.
May your Church today be filled with such different people,
united by the cross,
and celebrating our unity in your Son
with all your saints in glory.

Lord of the Church,
**hear our prayer,
and make us one in heart and mind
to serve you in Christ our Lord.   Amen.**                    3 C 2

See also the Intercession for Palm Sunday on page 83 of *Lent, Holy
Week, Easter*, which is suitable throughout this season.

## Acclamation

Christ became obedient unto death for us:
**even death upon a cross.**
He was pierced for our sins:
**bruised for no fault but our own.**
His punishment has brought us peace:
**and by his wounds we are healed.**
Worthy is the Lamb that was slain
to receive power and riches and wisdom:
**strength, honour, glory, and praise.   Amen.**                3 D 1

## Simple Blessing

Christ crucified draw you to himself,
to find in him a sure ground for faith,
a firm support for hope,
and the assurance of sins forgiven;
and the blessing . . .                                         3 E 1

# Solemn Blessing

You believe that by his dying
Christ destroyed death for ever.   **Amen.**

You have been crucified with Christ
and live by faith in the Son of God,
who loved you and gave himself for you.   **Amen.**

May he send you out to glory in his cross,
and live no longer for yourselves but for him,
who died and was raised to life for us.   **Amen.**

And the blessing . . .                                                3 F 1


## THE EUCHARIST

# Introduction to the Peace

Now in union with Christ Jesus
you who were once far off have been brought
near through the shedding of Christ's blood;
for he is our peace.                                                    3 G 1


# Eucharistic Preface

1    And now we give you thanks
because for our sins he was lifted high upon the cross,
that he might draw the whole world to himself;
and, by his suffering and death,
became the source of eternal salvation
for all who put their trust in him.
Therefore . . .                                                        3 H 1

2 And now we give you thanks
because for our salvation
he was obedient even to death on the cross.
The tree of shame was made the tree of glory;
and where life was lost, there life has been restored.
Therefore . . .                                                   *3 H 2*

3 And now we give you thanks
because, though he was sinless, he suffered willingly for sinners.
Though innocent, he accepted death to save the guilty.
By his dying he has destroyed our sins.
By his rising, he has raised us to holiness of life.
Therefore . . .                                                   *3 H 3*

4 And now we give you thanks
because Christ is the victim who dies no more,
the Lamb, once slain, who lives for ever,
our advocate in heaven to plead our cause,
exalting us there to join the angels and archangels,
for ever praising you and saying
**Holy, holy, holy Lord . . .**                               *3 H 4*

## *Words at the Breaking of Bread*

We break this bread,
**communion in Christ's body once broken.**

Let your Church be the wheat
which bears its fruit in dying.
**If we have died with him,
we shall live with him;
if we hold firm,
we shall reign with him.**                                    *3 J 1*

## *Invitation to Communion*

Jesus is the Lamb of God who takes away the sins of the world.
Happy are those who are called to his supper.
**Lord, I am not worthy to receive you,**
**but only say the word and I shall be healed.**        *3 K 1*

## *Prayers after Communion*

1    Lord, we have celebrated the memorial
          of your Son's eternal sacrifice.
     By his passion guard and defend us;
     by his wounds heal us;
     by his blood wash us from sin;
     by his death bring us to everlasting life and glory;
     for in him is the fulfilment of our hopes and longings,
     now and for ever.   **Amen.**        *3 L 1*

2    Lord God, whose Son is the true vine and the source of life,
     ever giving himself that the world might live;
     may we so receive within ourselves
          the power of his death and passion,
     that, in the cup of his life,
          we may share his glory and be made perfect in his love;
     for he is alive and reigns with you and the Holy Spirit,
     now and for ever.   **Amen.**        *3 L 2*

3    Faithful God,
     may we who share this banquet
     glory in the cross of our Lord Jesus Christ,
     our salvation, life and hope,
     who reigns as Lord now and for ever.   **Amen.**        *3 L 3*

## DAILY PRAYER

# *Light Prayer*

> Blessed are you, Sovereign God, gracious and merciful,
> you deal gently with those who go astray,
> and call those in darkness into the light of your presence.
> In the path of suffering Jesus learned obedience;
> With us as a brother he faced testing without sin;
> On a hill of darkness he carried judgement for the world;
> Merciful and faithful High Priest in the realm of light,
> he is strong to save all who draw near through him.
> Through the eternal Spirit he awakens us to serve you.
> Friend of sinners, Healer of the nations,
> Blessed are you, Sovereign God, who scatters the darkness.
> **Amen.**
>
> *3 M 1*

# *Canticles*

## 1 A SONG OF THE PASSION OF CHRIST

[Response **The steadfast love of the Lord never ceases.**]

1   Is it nothing to you all you who pass by:
   look and see if there is any sorrow like my sorrow.

2   Which was brought upon me whom the Lord inflicted:
   on the day of God's fierce anger.   **[R]**

3   For these things I weep; my eyes flow with tears:
   for a comforter is far from me, one to revive my courage.

4   Remember my affliction and my bitterness:
   the wormwood and the gall.   **[R]**

5   The steadfast love of the Lord never ceases:
   God's mercies never come to an end.

6   They are new every morning:
   great is your faithfulness, O God.   **[R]**

7    For you are my portion, says my soul:
     therefore will I hope in you.

8    You are good to those who wait for you:
     to the soul that seeks you.  **[R]**

9    It is good that one should wait quietly:
     for the salvation of God.

10   For you will not cast us off for ever:
     though we cause you grief, you will have compassion.

11   According to the abundance of your steadfast love:
     you do not willingly afflict or grieve us.  **[R]**      *3 N 1*

## 2  A SONG OF CHRIST THE SERVANT

[Response **We die to sin
and live to righteousness.**]

1    Christ suffered for you leaving you an example:
     that you should follow in his steps.

2    Christ committed no sin, no guile was found on his lips:
     when he was reviled, he did not revile in turn.  **[R]**

3    When he suffered, he did not threaten:
     but he trusted in God who judges justly.

4    Christ himself bore our sins in his body on the tree:
     that we might die to sin and live to righteousness.  **[R]**

5    By his wounds you have been healed,
     for you were straying like sheep:
     but have now returned
     to the Shepherd and Guardian of your souls.  **[R]**     *3 N 2*

### 3 A SONG OF THE REDEEMER

[Response **I will recount the steadfast love of the Lord.**]

1   Who is this who comes from Edom:
    coming from Bozrah his garments stained crimson?

2   He that is glorious in his apparel:
    marching in the greatness of his strength.

3   'It is I, who announce that right has won the day:
    'It is I,' says the Lord, 'for I am mighty to save.'   **[R]**

4   Why is your clothing all red, O Lord:
    and your garments like one that treads in the wine-press?

5   'I have trodden the wine press alone:
    and from the people no one was with me.'   **[R]**

6   I will recount the steadfast love of the Lord:
    and the praises of the Lord most high.

7   All that he has done for us in his tenderness:
    and by his many acts of love.   **[R]**

8   For he said, 'Surely they are my people,
    my children who will not deal falsely':
    and he became our Saviour and our Deliverer.

9   He himself saved us by his love and pity:
    he lifted us up and carried us through all the days of old.   **[R]** *3 N 3*

## *Patterns of Readings with Psalms and Canticles*

## *1   Theme: The Triumph of the Cross*

1   Genesis 3.1–15
      Psalm 40.5–11

2   Isaiah 11.10–end
      Psalm 2

3    Isaiah 45.21–end
      Psalm 98

4    Isaiah 52.13–end; 53.10–12
      Canticle: A Song of the Redeemer (*3 N 3* above)

5    Galatians 6.14–18
      Psalm 66.15–end

6    1 Corinthians 1.18–23
      The Song of Christ's Glory (ASB page 67)

Gospel   John 12.31–36a                    *3 P 1*


## 2   *Theme: Lazarus*

### *particularly for use on Palm Sunday*

1    Genesis 49.33—50.8,14,22–end
      Psalm 16

2    1 Kings 17.17–end
      Psalm 30

3    2 Kings 4.8–37 (or 8–10,18–21,32–37)
      Psalm 17.1–8,16

4    Ezekiel 37.1–14
      Psalm 130

5    Job 14.1–14
      Psalm 124

6    Romans 8.8–11
      Psalm 143.1–11

Gospel   John 11.1–44 (or 1–7,17–44)          *3 P 2*

## *Ending*

May our Lord and Saviour Jesus Christ,
who for us was scourged, loaded with his cross, and crucified,
bless us and keep us for evermore.   **Amen.**                    *3 Q 1*

# 4  EASTERTIDE

The fifty days from Easter to Pentecost, 'The Great Fifty Days', are a unity. Easter, Ascension and Pentecost are not a succession of seasons, but Eastertide encompasses the three mysteries of the resurrection, the ascension and the coming of the Spirit. The Easter Greeting

> Alleluia! Christ is risen.
> **He is risen indeed. Alleluia!**

and the Easter Dismissal

> Go in peace to love and serve the Lord. Alleluia! Alleluia!
> **In the name of Christ. Alleluia! Alleluia!**

envelop each celebration through these fifty days and begin to give it its distinctive festal feel. As Eastertide goes on Ascension material becomes appropriate as Ascension Day approaches, and after that Pentecost material in the last nine days of the season leading up to Whitsunday itself. Nevertheless the straightforwardly resurrection material in this chapter remains suitable throughout the season.

## Invitation to Confession

1  Christ our passover lamb has been offered for us.
Let us then rejoice by putting away all malice and evil
and confessing our sins with a sincere and true heart.        *4 A 1*

2  Christ died to sin once for all, and now he lives to God.
Let us renew our resolve to have done with all that is evil
and confess our sins in penitence and faith.        *4 A 2*

## Penitential Kyrie

Lord Jesus, you raise us to new life:
Lord, have mercy.
**Lord, have mercy.**

Lord Jesus, you forgive us our sins:
Christ, have mercy.
**Christ, have mercy.**

Lord Jesus, you feed us with the living bread:
Lord, have mercy.
**Lord, have mercy.**                                    4 B 1


## Intercession

1    In joy and hope let us pray to the Father, saying
**in Christ our Lord.**

That our risen Saviour may fill us (and . . . ) with the joy of his
     glorious and life-giving resurrection . . .
let us pray to the Father
**in Christ our Lord.**

That isolated and persecuted churches may find fresh strength
     in the good news of Easter . . .
let us pray to the Father
**in Christ our Lord.**

That God may grant us humility to be subject to one another
     in Christian love . . .
let us pray to the Father
**in Christ our Lord.**

That he may provide for those who lack food, work, or
     shelter . . .
let us pray to the Father
**in Christ our Lord.**

That by his power war and famine may cease through all the
world . . .
let us pray to the Father
**in Christ our Lord.**

That he may reveal the light of his presence to the sick, the
weak, and the dying to comfort and strengthen them . . .
let us pray to the Father
**in Christ our Lord.**

That, according to his promises,
all who have died in the faith of the resurrection
may rejoice in eternal life . . .
let us pray to the Father
**in Christ our Lord.**

That he may send forth the fire of the Holy Spirit upon his
people, so that we may bear faithful witness to his resurrection,
let us pray to the Father
**in Christ our Lord.**

Heavenly Father,
you have delivered us from the power of darkness
and brought us into the kingdom of your Son:
grant that, as his death has recalled us to life,
so his continual presence in us may raise us to eternal joy;
through Christ our Lord.   **Amen.**                          *4 C 1*

2    We pray to Jesus who is present with us to eternity, saying
Jesus, Lord of life,
**in your mercy, hear us.**

Jesus, light of the world,
bring the light and peace of your gospel to the nations . . .

Jesus, Lord of life,
**in your mercy, hear us.**

Jesus, bread of life,
give food to the hungry . . .
and nourish us all with your word.

Jesus, Lord of life,
**in your mercy, hear us.**

Jesus, our way, our truth, our life,
be with us and all who follow you in the way . . .
deepen our appreciation of your truth,
and fill us with your life.

Jesus, Lord of life,
**in your mercy, hear us.**

Jesus, good shepherd who gave your life for the sheep,
recover the straggler, bind up the injured,
strengthen the sick
and lead the healthy and strong to play.

Jesus, Lord of life,
**in your mercy, hear us.**

Jesus, the resurrection and the life,
we give you thanks
for all who have lived and believed in you . . .
raise us with them to eternal life.

Jesus, Lord of life,
**in your mercy, hear us,
accept our prayers,
and be with us always.   Amen.**                          *4 C 2*

See also the Easter Intercession on page 278 of *Lent, Holy Week,
Easter*.

## *Acclamation*

1   Alleluia! Christ is risen.
    **He is risen indeed. Alleluia!**
    Praise the God and Father of our Lord Jesus Christ.
    **He has given us new life and hope!**
    **He has raised Jesus from the dead!**
    God has claimed us as his own.
    **He has brought us out of darkness!**
    **He has made us light to the world!**
    Alleluia! Christ is risen.
    **He is risen indeed. Alleluia!**                       *4 D 1*

2   Here are words you may trust.
    Remember Jesus Christ, risen from the dead:
    **he is our salvation, our eternal glory.**
    If we die with him, we shall live with him:
    **if we endure we shall reign with him.**
    If we deny him, he will deny us:
    **if we are faithless, he keeps faith.**
    For he has broken the power of death:
    **and brought life and immortality to light**
        **through the gospel.**                             *4 D 2*

## *Simple Blessing*

1   The God of peace,
    who brought again from the dead our Lord Jesus,
    that great shepherd of the sheep,
    through the blood of the eternal covenant,
    make you perfect in every good work to do his will,
    working in you that which is well-pleasing in his sight;
    and the blessing . . .                                  *4 E 1*

2    God the Father,
by whose glory Christ was raised from the dead,
strengthen you to walk with him in his risen life;
and the blessing . . .        *4 E 2*

3    God, who through the resurrection of our Lord Jesus Christ
      has given us the victory,
give you joy and peace in your faith;
and the blessing . . .        *4 E 3*

4    May Christ,
who out of defeat brings new hope and a new future,
fill you with his new life;
and the blessing . . .        *4 E 4*

## Solemn Blessing

God the Father,
by whose love Christ was raised from the dead,
open to you who believe the gate of everlasting life.  **Amen.**

God the Son,
who in bursting the grave has won a glorious victory,
give you joy as you share the Easter faith.  **Amen.**

God the Holy Spirit,
whom the risen Lord breathed into his disciples,
empower you and fill you with Christ's peace.  **Amen.**

And the blessing . . .        *4 F 1*

## THE EUCHARIST

## Introduction to the Peace

The risen Christ came and stood among his disciples and said,
Peace be with you.
Then were they glad when they saw the Lord.    *4 G 1*

## *Eucharistic Preface*

1   And now we give you thanks
    because you raised him gloriously from the dead.
    For he is the true Paschal Lamb who was offered for us
    and has taken away the sin of the world.
    By his death he has destroyed death,
    and by his rising he has restored to us eternal life.
    Therefore . . .                                           *4 H 1*

2   And now we give you thanks
    because in his victory over the grave a new age has dawned,
    the long reign of sin is ended,
    a broken world is being renewed,
    and humanity is once again made whole.
    Therefore . . .                                           *4 H 2*

3   And now we give you thanks
    because through him you have given us eternal life,
    and delivered us from the bondage of sin and the fear of death
    into the glorious liberty of the children of God.
    Therefore . . .                                           *4 H 3*

4   And now we give you thanks
     because Christ our paschal sacrifice
        has made us children of the light,
    rising to new and everlasting life.
    He has opened the gates of heaven
    to receive his faithful people.
    His death is our ransom from death:
    his resurrection is our rising to life.
    The joy of the resurrection renews the whole world,
    while the choirs of heaven sing for ever to your glory
    **Holy, holy, holy Lord . . .**                           *4 H 4*

See also prefaces in *Patterns for Worship*.

## Words at the Breaking of Bread

Lord, we died with you on the cross.
**Now we are raised to new life.**
We were buried in your tomb.
**Now we share in your resurrection.**
Live in us, that we may live in you.                    4 J 1

## Invitation to Communion

Alleluia! Christ our Passover is sacrificed for us.
**Alleluia! Let us keep the feast.**                    4 K 1

## Prayers after Communion

1    God of truth,
     we have seen with our eyes
     and touched with our hands
     the bread of life.
     Strengthen our faith
     that we may grow in love for you
     and for each other;
     through Jesus Christ our Lord.    **Amen.**            4 L 1

2    Father, your risen Son was recognized by his disciples
         in the breaking of bread;
     through the power of this blessed sacrament of your presence
     may we abide in him and he in us;
     for he is alive and reigns for ever.    **Amen.**        4 L 2

3   God of our salvation,
    you have restored us to life,
    you have brought us back again into your love,
    by the triumphant death and resurrection of Christ:
    continue to heal us,
    as we go to live and work
    in the power of your Spirit,
    to your praise and glory.   **Amen.**                    *4 L 3*

This prayer should not be used if 'Almighty God, we thank you
. . .' is to be used, since the second part of each is so similar.
As a congregational prayer it might appropriately replace it.

4   O Lord,
    who by triumphing over the power of darkness
    prepared our place in the new Jerusalem:
    grant that we, who have this day
        given thanks for your resurrection,
    may praise you in the city where you are the light;
    for there with the Father and the Holy Spirit
    you live and reign, now and for ever.   **Amen.**        *4 L 4*

This prayer is suitable only at an evening eucharist.

The ASB prayer, 'Father of all, we give you thanks and praise . . .',
is suitable throughout Eastertide, whether as a presidential or a
congregational text. As the latter it might replace 'Almighty God,
we thank you . . .' throughout the season.

## DAILY PRAYER

# *Light Prayer*

> Blessed are you, Sovereign God, Conqueror of death,
> your light invades the places of darkness,
> restores sight and joy to the blind,
> and summons those enslaved by death to walk free in hope.
> For us Jesus poured out his life like water,
> and lay bound in the dusk of death.
> In his rising a new world is created,
> where light, goodness and joy spring forth.
> The rule of sin is broken for ever;
> love and truth drive out hatred and folly;
> a new humanity is clothed with your love
> and sings with hope of beauty to come.
> Joy of those who walk in darkness,
> Destroyer of death, Hope of resurrection,
> blessed are you, Sovereign God, Light of the World.
> **Amen.**
>
> *4 M 1*

# *Canticles*

### 1 THE SONG OF MOSES

[Response **The Lord is my strength and my song.**]

1     I will sing to the Lord, for he has triumphed gloriously:
     he has thrown the horse and its rider into the sea.

2     The Lord is my strength and my song:
     and he has become my salvation.   **[R]**

3     This is my God, and I will praise him:
     the God of my fathers and I will exalt him.

4     Lord, who among the gods is like you:
     majestic in holiness and working wonders?

5    In your unfailing love you will lead the people you have
       redeemed:
    in your strength you will guide them to your holy
       dwelling.  **[R]**

6    You will bring them in and plant them on your mountain:
    the place you have made for your dwelling.

7    In the sanctuary that your hands have established:
    you, Lord, will reign for ever and ever.  **[R]**       *4 N 1*

## 2  A SONG OF FAITH

[Response  **Praise be to the God and Father of our Lord
Jesus Christ.**]

1    Praise be to the God and Father of our Lord Jesus Christ:
    who in his great mercy gave us a new birth as his children.

2    God has raised Jesus Christ from the dead:
    so that we have a sure hope in him.  **[R]**

3    We have the promise of an inheritance that can never spoil:
    because it is kept for us in heaven.

4    The ransom that was paid to free us:
    was not paid in silver or gold,

5    But in the precious blood of Christ:
    the Lamb without spot or stain.  **[R]**

6    God raised him from the dead and gave him glory:
    so that we might have faith and hope in God.  **[R]**    *4 N 2*

## *Patterns of Readings with Psalms and Canticles*

# *1*

1    Isaiah 25.1–9
    Psalm 113

2 Jeremiah 31.1–14
Psalm 116.1–9

3 Zephaniah 3.14–end
Psalm 118.1–9

4 Isaiah 42.11–16
Psalm 118.14–18

5 Zechariah 8.1–8
Psalm 118.19–28

6 Revelation 1.10–18
Te Deum Part 2

Gospel   John 21.1–14                                          *4 P 1*


## 2

1 Acts 5.17–32
Psalm 2

2 Acts 10.34–43
Psalm 111

3 Acts 13.26–41
Psalm 16.7–end

4 Acts 17.16–31
Psalm 138

5 Acts 26.1–23
Psalm 117

6 1 Corinthians 15.3–11
The Easter Anthems

Gospel   Luke 24.13–35                                         *4 P 2*

## *Ending*

[Let us bless the Lord. Alleluia! Alleluia!
**Thanks be to God. Alleluia! Alleluia!**]

Christ yesterday and today,
the beginning and the end,
Alpha and Omega,
all time belongs to him,
and all ages;
to him be glory and power,
through every age and for ever.   **Amen.**                    *4 Q 1*

# 5 ASCENSION

This material on the theme of the Ascension is suitable on the days before and after Ascension Day, as well as on the feast itself. Its use does not have to wait until Ascension. The Sunday before (Easter 5 in both BCP and ASB) begins to anticipate Ascension themes. In the ten days from Ascension Day to Pentecost, the material for the Holy Spirit should begin to be used (see note at the beginning of Chapter 6).

The days till Pentecost are still part of the Great Fifty Days of Easter. Easter material continues to be appropriate, and the **Alleluia** is added to sentences, dismissals, etc.

## Invitation to Confession

1   Seeing we have a great high priest
    who has passed into the heavens,
    Jesus the Son of God,
    let us draw near with a true heart,
    in full assurance of faith,
    and make our confession to our heavenly Father.        *5 A 1*

2   Jesus is our high priest,
    tempted like us, yet without sin.
    He lives for ever in heaven to intercede for us.
    Through him we approach the throne of grace with confidence,
    and confess our sins.        *5 A 2*

## Penitential Kyrie

Lord Jesus, you have shown us the way to the Father:
Lord, have mercy.
**Lord, have mercy.**

Lord Jesus, your word is a light to our path:
Christ, have mercy.
**Christ, have mercy.**

Lord Jesus, you are the Good Shepherd,
    leading us into everlasting life:
Lord, have mercy.
**Lord, have mercy.**                                    5 B 1

## Intercession

Let us join our prayers with those of our Saviour Christ, seeking
the Father's blessing and the gifts of the Spirit.

The response to the words 'Jesus Christ, pray to the Father' is
'Jesus Christ, send us the Spirit'.

Jesus Christ, pray to the Father.
**Jesus Christ, send us the Spirit.**

Jesus Christ, great high priest,
living for ever to intercede for us,
pray for the Church, your broken body in the world . . .

Jesus Christ, pray to the Father.
**Jesus Christ, send us the Spirit.**

Jesus Christ, king of righteousness,
enthroned at the right hand of the majesty on high,
pray for the world, and make it subject to your gentle rule . . .

Jesus Christ, pray to the Father.
**Jesus Christ, send us the Spirit.**

Jesus Christ, Son of Man,
drawing humanity into the life of God,
pray for your brothers and sisters in need, distress or
    sorrow . . .

Jesus Christ, pray to the Father.
**Jesus Christ, send us the Spirit.**

Jesus Christ, pioneer of our salvation,
bringing us to your glory through your death and resurrection.
receive into your kingdom
 those who have died trusting your promises . . .

Jesus Christ, pray to the Father.
**Jesus Christ, send us the Spirit.**

Jesus Christ, Lord of all things,
ascending far above the heavens and filling the universe,
pray for us who receive the gifts you give for work in your
 service . . .

Jesus Christ, pray to the Father.
**Jesus Christ, send us the Spirit.**

Jesus Christ, keep the Church in the unity of the Spirit
 and in the bond of your peace,
and bring the whole created order to worship at your feet;
for you are alive and reign with the Father and the Holy Spirit,
one God, now and for ever. **Amen.**   *5 C 1*

## *Acclamation*

[Christ has gone up on high.
**Alleluia!**]

God raised Christ from the dead
**and enthroned him at his right hand**
 **in the heavenly realms.**
God put all things in subjection beneath his feet
**and gave him as head over all things to the Church.**
We died, and our life lies hidden with Christ in God.
**We set our minds on things above.**
When Christ, who is our life, is revealed,
**then we too will be revealed with him in glory.**

[Christ has gone up on high.
**Alleluia!**]   *5 D 1*

## Simple Blessing

1   Christ our King make you faithful and strong to do his will,
that you may reign with him in glory;
and the blessing . . .                                    5 E 1

2   Christ our exalted King pour upon you his abundant gifts
and bring you to reign with him in glory;
and the blessing . . .                                    5 E 2

## Solemn Blessing

God the Father,
who has given to his Son the name above every name,
strengthen you to proclaim Christ Jesus as Lord.   **Amen.**

God the Son,
who is our great high priest passed into the heavens,
plead for you at the right hand of the Father.   **Amen.**

God the Holy Spirit,
who pours out his abundant gifts upon the Church,
make you faithful servants of Christ our king.   **Amen.**

And the blessing . . .                                    5 F 1

THE EUCHARIST

## Introduction to the Peace

Jesus says:
Peace is my parting gift to you,
my own peace, such as the world cannot give.
Trust in God always; trust also in me.                    5 G 1

## *Eucharistic Preface*

1   And now we give you thanks
because you have highly exalted him,
and given him the name which is above all other names,
that at the name of Jesus every knee shall bow.
Therefore . . .                                                          *5H1*

2   And now we give you thanks
because after his most glorious resurrection
he openly appeared to his disciples,
and in their sight ascended up into heaven
to prepare a place for us;
that where he is, there we might also be,
and reign with him in glory.
Therefore . . .                                                          *5H2*

3   And now we give you thanks
that he is the King of Glory,
who overcomes the sting of death
and opens the kingdom of heaven to all believers.
He is seated at your right hand in glory
and we believe that he will come to be our judge.
Therefore . . .                                                          *5H3*

4   Father, we are in your Spirit and we hear your voice:
'I am the first and the last, who is, who was,
    and who is to come.'
Before the worlds were made, Christ was alive.
Through him you created everything in heaven and on earth,
the whole universe created through him and for him.

[Lord of glory,
**we worship and adore you.**]

You sent him, the visible likeness
of the invisible God,
to reflect the brightness of your glory,
to sustain the universe with his word of power,
to achieve forgiveness for the sins of all.

[Lord of glory,
**we worship and adore you.**]

And now he rules in heaven, mighty risen Lord,
his voice like a roaring waterfall:
'I am the living one!
I was dead but now I am alive for ever and ever.'

[Lord of glory,
**we worship and adore you.**]

So, with angels and archangels,
and all the company of heaven,
we praise you for ever, saying
**Holy, holy, holy Lord . . .**

*5H4*

## Words at the Breaking of Bread

Lord, we died with you on the cross.
**Now we are raised to new life.**
We were buried in your tomb.
**Now we share in your resurrection.**
Live in us, that we may live in you.

*5J1*

## Invitation to Communion

1    I heard the voice of a great multitude crying, Alleluia!
        The Lord our God has entered into his kingdom.
    **Blessed are those who are called
        to the supper of the Lamb. Alleluia!**

*5K1*

2    Alleluia! Christ our Passover is sacrificed for us.
    **Alleluia! Let us keep the feast.**

*5K2*

## Prayers after Communion

1  O God our Father,
   you have raised our humanity in Christ
   and have fed us with the bread of heaven.
   Mercifully grant that with such spiritual blessings
   we may set our hearts in the heavenly places;
   through Jesus Christ our Lord.  **Amen.**                    *5 L 1*

2  Eternal Giver of love and power,
   your Son Jesus Christ has sent us into all the world
   to preach the gospel of his kingdom.
   Confirm us in this mission,
   and help us to live the good news we proclaim;
   through Jesus Christ our Lord.  **Amen.**                    *5 L 2*

DAILY PRAYER

## Light Prayer

Blessed are you, Sovereign God, reigning in glory.
Cloud and deep darkness proclaim your holiness;
radiant light shows forth your truth.
Jesus has entered the cloud of your presence;
he has taken his seat at the right hand of Majesty.
Perfect sacrifice, he has put away sins.
Merciful high priest, he pleads for our weakness.
Always our brother, he prepares our place in heaven.
Ruler of all, he establishes your reign.
Dawning light for the righteous, hope of sinners,
Blessed are you, Sovereign God, high over all.
**Amen.**                                                       *5 M 1*

# *Canticles*

## 1 A SONG OF REDEMPTION

[Response **Christ is the head of the body, the Church.**]

1 The Father has delivered us from the dominion of darkness:
and transferred us to the kingdom of his beloved Son.

2 In whom we have redemption:
the forgiveness of our sins. **[R]**

3 He is the image of the invisible God:
the first-born of all creation.

4 For'in him all things were created:
in heaven and on earth, visible and invisible.

5 All things were created through him and for him:
he is before all things
and in him all things hold together. **[R]**

6 He is the head of the body, the Church:
he is the beginning, the first-born from the dead.

7 For it pleased God that in him all fulness should dwell:
and that through him all things should be reconciled to
himself. **[R]**                                                   5 *N 1*

## 2 A SONG OF GOD'S GRACE

[Response **You have blessed us in Christ Jesus.**]

1 Blessed be the God and Father of our Lord Jesus Christ:
for you have blessed us in Christ Jesus
with every spiritual blessing in the heavenly places.

2 You chose us to be yours
before the foundation of the world:
that we should be holy and blameless in your sight. **[R]**

3 In love you destined us to be your children,
through Jesus Christ:
such was your pleasure and your purpose,

4    To the praise of your glorious grace:
     which you have freely given us in the Beloved.  **[R]**

5    We have redemption through the blood of Christ:
     the forgiveness of our sins,

6    According to the riches of the grace:
     which you have freely lavished upon us.  **[R]**

7    You have made known to us in all wisdom and insight:
     the mystery of your will,

8    According to your purpose
      which you revealed in Christ Jesus:
     as a plan for the fulness of time,

9    To unite all things in Christ:
     things in heaven and things on earth.  **[R]**        *5 N 2*

## *Patterns of Readings with Psalms and Canticles*

## *1  Theme: The Kingship and Priesthood of Christ*

1    Ezekiel 1.4–5, 26–end
     Bless the Lord (ASB page 65)

2    Zechariah 3
     Psalm 110

3    Daniel 7.9–14
     Psalm 21.1–6

4    Revelation 1.10–18
     Song of Christ's Glory (ASB page 67)

5    Revelation 3.14–end
     Song of the Lamb (*The Promise* page 332)

or

     Revelation 5.6–end
     Great and Wonderful (ASB page 54)

6    Hebrews 2.9–end
     A Song of Redemption (*5 N 1* above)

Gospel   A Luke 24.45–end
         B Matthew 28.16–end
         C Mark 16.14–end                          *5 P 1*


## 2   Theme: Parting Words

1    Abraham: Genesis 24.1–4,9; 25.7–10
     Psalm 105.1–9

2    Jacob: Genesis 49.1–2, 22–26,28–end
     Psalm 78.1–7

3    Moses: Deuteronomy 34
     Canticle: Deuteronomy 33.2–4,26–27a,29

4    David: 2 Samuel 2.1–4,10; 1 Samuel 23.1
     Canticle: 1 Samuel 23.2–5

5    Elijah: 2 Kings 2.1–15
     Psalm 15

6    Paul: 2 Timothy 1.1–7; 4.1–8
     A Song of God's Grace (*5 N 2* above)

Gospel   John 16.12–15, 25–end                     *5 P 2*


## Ending

Now to him who is able to do immeasurably more
    than we can ask or conceive,
by the power which is at work among us,
to him be glory in the Church and in Christ Jesus
throughout all ages.  **Amen.**                    *5 Q 1*

# 6 PENTECOST

This material is suitable for use on the Feast of Pentecost, Whitsunday, and on the days preceding it. It is not intended primarily for use after Pentecost Day itself, for Pentecost is the climax of the Great Fifty Days, rather than the beginning of a new season.

Because Pentecost is the last day of Easter, the Easter material continues to be appropriate as well as this more specifically Holy Spirit material. **Alleluia** is added to sentences, dismissals, etc. until Pentecost evening.

## Invitation to Confession

1    The Spirit of truth will convict the world of guilt
about sin, righteousness and judgement.
We have grieved the Holy Spirit.
We confess our sins in penitence and faith.       *6 A 1*

2    The Spirit of the Lord fills the world
and knows our every word and deed.
Let us then open ourselves to the Lord
and confess our sins in penitence and faith.       *6 A 2*

## Penitential Kyrie

You raise the dead to life in the Spirit:
Lord, have mercy.
**Lord, have mercy.**

You bring pardon and peace to the broken in heart:
Christ, have mercy.
**Christ, have mercy.**

You make one by your Spirit the torn and divided:
Lord, have mercy.
**Lord, have mercy.**       *6 B 1*

# *Intercession*

We pray for God to fill us with his Spirit, saying
Lord, come to bless us
**and fill us with your Spirit.**

Generous God,
we thank you for the *power* of your Holy Spirit.
We ask that we may be strengthened to serve you better.

Lord, come to bless us
**and fill us with your Spirit.**

We thank you for the *wisdom* of your Holy Spirit.
We ask you to help us understand better your will for us.

Lord, come to bless us
**and fill us with your Spirit.**

We thank you for the *peace* of your Holy Spirit.
We ask you to keep us confident of your love
    wherever you call us.

Lord, come to bless us
**and fill us with your Spirit.**

We thank you for the *healing* of your Holy Spirit.
We ask you to bring reconciliation and wholeness
    where there is division, sickness and sorrow.

Lord, come to bless us
**and fill us with your Holy Spirit.**

We thank you for the *gifts* of your Holy Spirit.
We ask you to equip us for the work which you have given us.

Lord, come to bless us
**and fill us with your Holy Spirit.**

We thank you for the *fruit* of your Holy Spirit.
We ask you to reveal in our lives the love of Jesus.

Lord, come to bless us
**and fill us with your Spirit.**

We thank you for the *breath* of your Holy Spirit given on Easter
Day.
We ask you to keep the whole Church, living and departed,
in the joy of eternal life.

Lord, come to bless us
**and fill us with your Spirit.**

Generous God,
you sent your Holy Spirit upon your Messiah at the river Jordan,
and upon the disciples in the upper room:
in your mercy fill us with your Spirit,
**hear our prayer,
and make us one in heart and mind
to serve you in Christ our Lord.   Amen.**                    *6 C 1*


## Acclamation

1    The love of God has been poured into our hearts,
through the Holy Spirit who has been given to us:
**we dwell in him and he in us.**
Give thanks to the Lord and call upon his name:
**make known his deeds among the peoples.**
Sing to him, sing praises to him:
**and speak of all his marvellous works.**
Holy, holy, holy is the Lord God almighty:
**who was and is and is to come!**                            *6 D 1*


2    For the last day of Easter:

Alleluia! Christ is risen.
**He is risen indeed. Alleluia!**
You that sleep, awake, rise from the dead. Alleluia!
**Christ our light will shine upon us. Alleluia!**
Christ has gone up on high. Alleluia!
**He has ascended to the heights of heaven. Alleluia!**

The Spirit of the Lord fills the whole universe. Alleluia!
**The Spirit of the Lord
   brings mighty things to pass. Alleluia!**                    *6 D 2*

## Simple Blessing

1    The Spirit of truth lead you into all truth,
     give you grace to confess that Jesus Christ is Lord,
     and to proclaim the word and works of God;
     and the blessing . . .                                     *6 E 1*

2    May the God of hope fill you
     with all joy and peace in believing,
     through the power of the Holy Spirit;
     and the blessing . . .                                     *6 E 2*

## Solemn Blessing

May the Spirit,
who hovered over the waters when the world was created,
breathe into you the life he gives.   **Amen.**

May the Spirit,
who overshadowed the Virgin
   when the eternal Son came among us,
make you joyful in the service of the Lord.   **Amen.**

May the Spirit,
who set the Church on fire upon the day of Pentecost,
bring the world alive with the love of the risen Christ.   **Amen.**

And the blessing . . .                                          *6 F 1*

## THE EUCHARIST

## *Introduction to the Peace*

The fruit of the Spirit is love, joy, peace.
If we live in the Spirit, let us walk in the Spirit. *6 G 1*


## *Eucharistic Preface*

1   And now we give you thanks
    because by the Holy Spirit you lead us into all truth,
    and give us power to proclaim your gospel to the nations,
    and to serve you as a royal priesthood.
    Therefore . . . *6 H 1*

2   And now we give you thanks
    because in fulfilment of your promise
    you pour your Spirit upon us,
    filling us with your gifts, leading us into all truth,
    and uniting peoples of many tongues
        in the confession of one faith.
    You give us power to proclaim your gospel to all nations
    and to serve you as a royal priesthood.
    Therefore we join our voices with angels and archangels,
    and with all those in whom the Spirit dwells,
    to proclaim the glory of your name,
    for ever praising you and saying
    **Holy, holy, holy Lord . . .** *6 H 2*

3   And now we give you thanks
    that after he had ascended up far above all heavens
    and was set down at the right hand of your majesty,
    he sent forth upon the universal Church
    your holy and life-giving Spirit:
    that through his glorious power
    the joy of the everlasting gospel
    might go forth into all the world,

bringing us out of darkness and error
into the clear light and true knowledge of you,
and of your Son our Saviour Jesus Christ.
Therefore . . .                                                                 *6 H 3*

See also the Thanksgivings in *Patterns for Worship*.

## Words at the Breaking of Bread

Lord, we died with you on the cross.
**Now we are raised to new life.**
We are buried in your tomb.
**Now we share in your resurrection.**
Live in us, that we may live in you.                              *6 J 1*

## Invitation to Communion

Alleluia! Christ our Passover is sacrificed for us.
**Alleluia! Let us keep the feast.**                              *6 K 1*

## Prayers after Communion

1    Almighty and everliving God,
     who fulfilled the promises of Easter
     by sending us your Holy Spirit
     and opening to every race and nation
     the way of life eternal,
     open our lips by your Spirit,
     that every tongue may tell of your glory;
     through Jesus Christ our Lord.   **Amen.**            *6 L 1*

2    God of power,
        may the boldness of your Spirit transform us,
        may the gentleness of your Spirit lead us,
        may the gifts of your Spirit equip us
          to serve and worship you
        now and always.  **Amen.**          *6 L 2*

The second collect for Pentecost in ASB is better used as a post-communion collect than at the beginning of the eucharist.

## DAILY PRAYER

### *Light Prayer*

Blessed are you, Sovereign God, overflowing in love.
Your Holy Spirit hovered over the unformed world,
overshadowed Mary when the Word took flesh,
and made ready the cleansing sacrifice of Calvary
so that the grain of wheat died to bear much fruit.
With the harvest of Pentecost dawns the age of the Spirit.
Now the flame of heaven rests on every believer;
the confusion of Babel melts into praise from all nations.
Strong and weak, women and men tell out your word;
the young receive visions, the old receive dreams.
With the new wine of the Spirit
they proclaim your amnesty of love.
Amid the birth pains of the new creation
the way of light is made known.
Source of freedom, giver of life,
blessed are you, Sovereign God, Light of the world.
**Amen.**          *6 M 1*

# *Canticles*

### 1 THE SONG OF JUDITH

[Response  **You sent forth your Spirit
and all things came to be.**]

1  I will sing a new song to my God:
for you are great and glorious,
truly strong and invincible.

2  May your whole creation serve you:
for you spoke and all things came to be.   **[R]**

3  You sent forth your Spirit and they were formed:
for no one can resist your voice.

4  Mountains and seas are stirred to their depths:
at your presence rocks shall melt like wax.   **[R]**

5  For every sacrifice, as a fragrant offering,
is a small thing:
but whoever reveres you shall be great for ever.   **[R]**   *6 N 1*

### 2  A SONG OF EZEKIEL

[Response  **I will put a new spirit within you.**]

1  I will take you from the nations:
and gather you from all the countries.

2  I will sprinkle clean water upon you:
and purify you from all defilement.   **[R]**

3  A new heart I will give you:
and put a new spirit within you.

4  I will take from your body the heart of stone:
and give you a heart of flesh.

5  You shall be my people:
and I will be your God.   **[R]**   *6 N 2*

## Patterns of Readings with Psalms and Canticles

## 1  Theme: The Coming Spirit

1  Deuteronomy 34
   Canticle: Deuteronomy 33.2–4,26–27a,29

2  2 Samuel 2.1–4,10; 1 Samuel 23.1
   Canticle: 1 Samuel 23.2–5

3  2 Kings 2.1–15 or 9–15
   Psalm 108.1–5

4  Isaiah 64.1–7
   Song of the New Creation (*The Promise* page 314)

5  Revelation 21.1–4,10,22–end; 22.1–5
   A Song of the Spirit (*The Promise* page 333)

6  Ephesians 4.7–13
   Psalm 68.2–6,18,32–end

Gospel   John 17.1–11                                      *6 P 1*


## 2  Theme: The Spirit in Acts

1  Acts 3.1–16 and/or 4.5–12
   Psalm 139.1–6,12–17

2  Acts 5.12–32 or 17–32
   Psalm 51.6–13

3  Acts 8.5–8, 14–17
   Psalm 68.3–4,32–34

4  Acts 10.34–end
   Psalm 33.1–6,20–21

5  Acts 18.24—19.7
   Psalm 104.1–2,32–36

6     1 Corinthians 2.1–13
         Psalm 143.1–2,5–8,10

Gospel   John 15.26—16.7                                          *6 P 2*


## *Ending*

> May the love of the Father enfold us,
> the wisdom of the Son enlighten us,
> the fire of the Spirit kindle us;
> and may the blessing of the Lord God
>     come down upon us
>     and remain with us always.   **Amen.**        *6 Q 1*

# 7 TRINITY SUNDAY

## Invitation to Confession

1 Holy, holy, holy.
  When our eyes have seen the Lord of hosts
   we echo the words of Isaiah,
  'Woe is me! I am doomed'.
  We long for the fire of God's cleansing
   to touch our unclean lips,
  for our iniquity to be removed and our sins wiped out.
  So we meet Father, Son and Holy Spirit
   with confession on our lips.       *7 A 1*

This Invitation should not be combined with 7 *B* 2 below.

2 'How often have I longed to gather your children,
  as a hen gathers her brood under her wings,' says the Lord,
  'but you would not let me.'
  Let us as wayward children return to God
   and confess our sins.         *7 A 2*

This Invitation relates directly to 7 *B* 3 below which reflects upon Matthew 23.37.

## Penitential Kyrie

1 Father, you come to meet us when we return to you:
  Lord, have mercy.
  **Lord, have mercy.**

  Jesus, you died on the cross for our sins:
  Christ, have mercy.
  **Christ, have mercy.**

  Spirit, you give us life and peace:
  Lord, have mercy.
  **Lord, have mercy.**         *7 B 1*

2     Holy, holy, holy is the Lord of hosts;
       the whole earth is full of his glory:
    Lord, have mercy.
**Lord, have mercy.**

Woe is me, for I am lost; I am a person of unclean lips:
Christ, have mercy.
**Christ, have mercy.**

Your guilt is taken away, and your sin forgiven:
Lord, have mercy.
**Lord, have mercy.**              *7 B 2*

3     Father, you enfold us with wings of love,
       as a bird protects her young.
    In our sin we have spurned your love.
    Lord, have mercy.
**Lord, have mercy.**

Jesus, you gather us around you that we may learn your ways.
In our sin we have strayed from your presence.
Christ, have mercy.
**Christ, have mercy.**

Holy Spirit, you feed us with the seed of your holy word:
In our sin we have chosen the chaff.
Lord, have mercy.
**Lord, have mercy.**              *7 B 3*

## *Intercession*

We come boldly to the throne of grace,
    praying to the almighty God, Father, Son and Holy Spirit
    for mercy and grace, saying
**we plead before your throne in heaven.**

Father of heaven, whose love profound
  a ransom for our souls has found:
We pray for the world, created by your love,
  for its nations and governments . . .
Extend to them your peace, pardoning love, mercy and grace.
**We plead before your throne in heaven.**

Almighty Son, incarnate Word,
  our Prophet, Priest, Redeemer, Lord:
We pray for the Church, created for your glory,
for its ministry to reflect those works of yours . . .
Extend to us your salvation, growth, mercy and grace.
**We plead before your throne in heaven.**

Eternal Spirit, by whose breath
  the soul is raised from sin and death:
We pray for families and individuals, created in your image,
  for the lonely, the bereaved, the sick and the dying . . .
Breathe on them the breath of life and bring them to your mercy
  and grace.
**We plead before your throne in heaven.**

Mysterious Godhead, three in one,
  Jehovah – Father, Spirit, Son:
We pray for ourselves,
  for your Church, for all whom we remember before you . . .
Bring us all to bow before your throne in heaven,
  to receive life and pardon, mercy and grace for all eternity
  as we worship you, saying
**Holy, holy, holy Lord,**
**God of power and might,**
**heaven and earth are full of your glory.**
**Hosanna in the highest.   Amen.**                    7C1

## *Acclamation*

You are worthy, our Lord and God:
**to receive glory and honour and power.**
For you created all things:
**and through your will they have their being.**
You are worthy, Lamb of God, for you were slain:
**and by your blood you ransomed us for God.**
From every tribe and tongue and people and nation:
**you made us a kingdom of priests to serve our God.**
To him who sits upon the throne and to the Lamb
**be blessing and honour, glory and might**
   **for ever and ever. Amen.**         7 D 1

## *Simple Blessing*

God the Holy Trinity make you strong in faith and love,
defend you on every side,
and guide you in truth and peace;
and the blessing . . .         7 E 1

## *Solemn Blessing*

1    God the Father,
who first loved us and made us accepted in the beloved Son,
bless you. **Amen.**

God the Son,
who loved us and washed us from our sins in his own blood,
bless you. **Amen.**

God the Holy Spirit,
who sheds abroad the love of God in our hearts,
bless you. **Amen.**

The blessing of the one true God,
to whom be all love and all glory for time and for eternity,
come down upon you and remain with you always. **Amen.**
        7 F 1

2     The Lord bless you and keep you.   **Amen.**

The Lord make his face to shine upon you,
and be gracious to you.   **Amen.**

The Lord lift up his countenance upon you
and give you peace.   **Amen.**

The Lord God almighty, Father, Son, and Holy Spirit,
the holy and undivided Trinity,
guard you, save you,
and bring you to that heavenly city,
where he lives and reigns for ever and ever.   **Amen.**          7 F 2


## THE EUCHARIST

## *Introduction to the Peace*

Peace to you from God our heavenly Father.
Peace from his Son Jesus Christ who is our peace.
Peace from the Holy Spirit the Life-giver.
The peace of the triune God be always with you
**and also with you.**                                                    7 G 1


## *Eucharistic Preface*

1     And now we give you thanks
because you have revealed your glory
    as the glory of your Son and of the Holy Spirit:
three persons equal in majesty, undivided in splendour,
yet one Lord, one God, ever to be worshipped and adored.
Therefore . . .                                                          7 H 1

2     And now we give you thanks, most gracious God,
surrounded by a great cloud of witnesses
and glorified in the assembly of your saints.
(The glorious company of apostles praise you.

The noble fellowship of prophets praise you.
The white-robed army of martyrs praise you.)
We, your holy Church, acclaim you
Father of majesty unbounded,
    your true and only Son worthy of all worship,
    and the Holy Spirit advocate and guide.
Therefore with angels and all the powers of heaven,
with cherubim and seraphim, we sing in endless praise
**Holy, holy, holy Lord . . .**

*7H2*

## Words at the Breaking of Bread

'I am the bread which has come down from heaven',
    says the Lord.
**Give us this bread for ever.**
'I am the vine, you are the branches.'
**May we dwell in him, as he lives in us.**

*7J1*

## Invitation to Communion

The gifts of God for the people of God.
**Jesus Christ is holy,**
**Jesus Christ is Lord,**
**to the glory of God the Father.**

*7K1*

## Prayers after Communion

1    O God our mystery,
    you bring us to life,
    call us to freedom,
    and move between us with love.
    May we so participate
    in the dance of your trinity,
    that our lives may resonate with you,
    now and for ever. **Amen.**

*7L1*

2    Strengthen for service, Lord,
        the hands that have taken holy things;
     may the ears which have heard your word
        be deaf to clamour and dispute;
     may the tongues which have sung your praise
        be free from deceit;
     may the eyes which have seen the tokens of your love
        shine with the light of hope;
     and may the bodies which have been fed with your body
        be refreshed with the fulness of your life;
     glory to you for ever. **Amen.**                           *7 L 2*


## DAILY PRAYER

## *Light Blessing*

     We praise and thank you, O God,
     for you are without beginning and without end.
     Through Christ you are the creator and preserver
     of the whole world:
     but, above all, you are his God and Father,
     the giver of the Spirit,
     and the ruler of all that is, seen and unseen.
     You made the day for the works of light
     and the night for the refreshment of our minds and bodies.
     O loving Lord and source of all that is good,
     accept our evening sacrifice of praise.
     As you have led us through the day
     and brought us to night's beginning,
     keep us now in Christ;
     grant us a peaceful evening
     and a night free from sin;
     and, at the end, bring us to everlasting life.
     Through Christ and in the Holy Spirit,
     we offer you all glory, honour and worship,
     now and for ever.    **Amen.**                             *7 M 1*

See also the Light Prayer for Baptism (*17 M 1*).

# *Canticles*

## 1 A SONG OF GOD'S LOVE

[Response **We love because God first loved us.**]

1   Let us love one another:
    for love is from God.

2   Those who love are born of God and know God:
    but those who do not love
        know nothing of God; for God is love.   **[R]**

3   Those who dwell in love:
    are dwelling in God and God in them.

4   There is no room for fear in love:
    love which is perfected banishes fear.   **[R]**

5   If we do not love those whom we have seen:
    we cannot love God whom we have not seen.

6   This commandment we have from God:
    that those who love God must also love their neighbour.   **[R]**

*7N1*

## 2 PRAISE TO GOD THE HOLY TRINITY

The three parts can be divided in different ways, e.g. 1 = leader,
2 = women, 3 = men.

[Response **Glory to God, Father, Son and Holy Spirit.**]

1   Glory to the Holy and undivided Trinity;
2   Father, Son and Holy Spirit;
3   three persons and one God.

1   Perfectly one from before time began;
2   one in being and one in glory;
3   dwelling in love; three persons, one God.

1    Incarnate Son, in suffering forsaken;
2    Father, giving and forgiving;
3    Spirit, bond in joy and pain.

1    Eternal Father, the Fountain of Life;
2    Risen Son, the Prince of Life;
3    Spirit of freedom, Giver of Life.

1    Truth, Word and Power;
2    Lover, Beloved and Friend;
3    Hope without end; Joy beyond words.

**Glory to God, Father, Son and Holy Spirit.**          7 N 2


## Pattern of Readings, Psalms and Canticle

1    Genesis 1.1—2.3 or
     Genesis 1.26—2.3
        Psalm 8

2    Exodus 3.1–6
        Psalm 29

3    Isaiah 6.1–8
        Psalm 67

4    Job 38.1–11; 42.1–5
        Psalm 33.1–12

5    Ecclesiasticus 42.15–23; 43.27–33
        Psalm 93

6    Revelation 4.1–11
        Canticle: A Song of God's Grace (*The Promise* page 329)

Gospel    John 3.1–9 (10–15)                            7 P 1

## *Ending*

Blessing and honour and thanksgiving and praise,
more than we can utter, more than we can conceive,
be to you, most holy and glorious Trinity,
Father, Son and Holy Spirit,
by all angels, all people, all creatures,
for ever and ever.   **Amen.**                     7 Q 1

# 8 THE TRANSFIGURATION

## Invitation to Confession

When Christ appears we shall be like him,
because we shall see him as he is.
As he is pure,
all who have grasped this hope makes themselves pure.
So let us confess our sins that mar his image in us.          *8 A 1*

## Penitential Kyrie

Your unfailing kindness, O Lord, is in the heavens,
and your faithfulness reaches to the clouds:
Lord, have mercy.
**Lord, have mercy.**

Your righteousness is like the strong mountains,
and your justice as the great deep:
Christ, have mercy.
**Christ, have mercy.**

For with you is the well of life:
and in your light shall we see light:
Lord, have mercy.
**Lord, have mercy.**                                         *8 B 1*

## Intercession

Lord of glory, it is good that we are here.
In peace we make our prayer to you.
In trust we confirm our faith in you.
Help us to set our faces steadfastly where you would go with us.

Lord, look with favour.
**Lord, transfigure and heal.**

Lord of glory, look with favour on your Church,
proclaiming your beloved Son to the world
and listening to the promptings of his Spirit . . .
May it be renewed in holiness that it may reflect your glory.

Lord, look with favour.
**Lord, transfigure and heal.**

Lord of glory, look with favour on the nations of the world,
scarred by hatred, strife and war,
and crying out to be changed by the touch of your hand . . .
May they hear the good news like a lamp shining in a murky
place.

Lord, look with favour.
**Lord, transfigure and heal.**

Lord of glory, look with favour on those in need and distress,
suffering as your Son has suffered
and waiting for the salvation you promise . . .
May the day break
and Christ the Morning Star bring them the light of his
presence.

Lord, look with favour.
**Lord, transfigure and heal.**

Lord of glory, it is good if we suffer with you
  so that we shall be glorified with you.
According to your promise bring all Christ's brothers and
  sisters . . .
to see him with their own eyes in majesty
and to be changed into his likeness from glory to glory.

To him be praise, dominion and worship
now and for all eternity.  **Amen.**                          *8 C 1*

## Acclamation

By the appearance on earth of our Saviour Jesus Christ
**God has broken the power of death**
**and brought life and immortality to light.**

Arise, shine, for your light has come
**and the glory of the Lord has risen upon you.**
For though darkness shall cover the earth
**and thick darkness the nations,**
The Lord will rise upon you
**and his glory will be seen upon you.**

By the appearance on earth of our Saviour Jesus Christ
**God has broken the power of death**
**and brought life and immortality to light.** *8 D 1*

## Simple Blessing

Christ Jesus,
the splendour of the Father and the image of his being,
draw you to himself
that you may live in his light and share his glory;
and the blessing . . . *8 E 1*

## Solemn Blessing

Christ, whose glory fills the skies,
fill you with radiance
    and scatter the darkness from your path. **Amen.**

Christ, the Sun of Righteousness,
gladden your eyes and warm your heart. **Amen.**

Christ, the Dayspring from on high,
draw near to guide your feet into the way of peace. **Amen.**

And the blessing . . . *8 F 1*

THE EUCHARIST

## *Introduction to the Peace*

> Christ will transfigure our human body
> and give it a form like that of his own glorious body.
> We are the Body of Christ.
> We share his peace.
> The peace of the Lord be always with you . . .  *8 G 1*

## *Eucharistic Preface*

1  And now we give you thanks
because the divine glory of the incarnate Word
shone forth upon the holy mountain;
and your own voice from heaven proclaimed your beloved Son.
Therefore . . .  *8 H 1*

2  And now we give you thanks
because he revealed his glory to the disciples
to strengthen them for the scandal of the cross.
His glory shone from a body like our own,
to show that the Church,
which is the body of Christ,
would one day share his glory.
Therefore . . .  *8 H 2*

## *Words at the Breaking of Bread*

> We break the bread of life
> and that life is the light of the world:
> **God here among us,**
> **light in the midst of us,**
> **bring us to light and life.**  *8 J 1*

## Invitation to Communion

> The gifts of God for the people of God.
> **Jesus Christ is holy,**
> **Jesus Christ is Lord,**
> **to the glory of God the Father.** *8 K 1*

## Prayers after Communion

1 Holy God,
  we see your glory in the face of Jesus Christ.
  May we who are partakers of his table
  reflect his life in word and deed,
  that all the world may know
  his power to change and save.
  We ask this in his name,
  Jesus Christ our Lord.   **Amen.** *8 L 1*

2 Assist us, gracious Lord,
  as we listen to the voice of your Son;
  that as we now meet him under a veil,
  so we may come to the vision of his glory;
  through Jesus Christ our Lord.   **Amen.** *8 L 2*

DAILY PRAYER

## *Light Blessing*

Blessed are you, Sovereign God, enthroned in majesty,
Giver of freedom, unveiler of light;
your Spirit opens our eyes to your glory,
uncovers the faces of those shamed by sin,
and wonderfully transforms the weakness of our nature
that we may bear the image of the risen Christ.
On the mount of transfiguration
you bore witness to your Son,
revealed the glory of his being,
the urgent authority of his teaching
and his call as the kingly servant
who would liberate your people by his death.
In suffering the Spirit of glory rests upon us;
in worship the Spirit of love makes us free;
in the new age your glory shall be shown forth in us.
Tender in mercy, awesome in holiness,
blessed are you, Sovereign God, giver of glory.   **Amen.**   *8 M 1*

## *Canticles*

1   Te Deum 1–13 (ASB page 55)

2   Song of Redemption (see *5 N 1*)

## Pattern of Readings with Psalms and Canticles

1     Genesis 22.1–18
       Psalm 116.11–end

2     Exodus 24.12–18
       Psalm 84.8–end

3     1 Kings 19.1–16
       Psalm 2 or 99

4     2 Corinthians 3.1–9,18
       Psalm 89.5–18

5     2 Corinthians 4.1–6
       Psalm 72.1–8

6     2 Timothy 1.8–10
       Canticle: A Song of Redemption (*5 N 1* above)

Gospel   John 12.27–36a                    *8 P 1*

## Ending

    Now to him who is able
       through the power which is at work among us
    to do immeasurably more than we can ask or conceive,
    to him be glory in the Church and in Christ Jesus
    from generation to generation for evermore.   **Amen.**   *8 Q 1*

# 9  MICHAELMAS

## Invitation to Confession

We have come to Mount Zion,
the city of the living God,
the heavenly Jerusalem,
to myriads of angels,
to God the judge of all,
and to Jesus the mediator of a new covenant.
Let us confess our sins in penitence and faith.

*9 A 1*

## Penitential Kyrie

Holy, holy, holy is the Lord of hosts;
the whole earth is full of his glory.
Lord, have mercy.
**Lord, have mercy.**

Woe is me, for I am lost;
I am a person of unclean lips.
Christ, have mercy.
**Christ, have mercy.**

Your guilt is taken away,
and your sin forgiven.
Lord, have mercy.
**Lord, have mercy.**

*9 B 1*

## *Intercession*

Father in heaven,
by his blood your Christ has ransomed us to you,
and has made us a kingdom and priests to you our God.
As the angels minister to you in heaven,
strengthen your Church to serve you here on earth.

Lord, hear us.
**Lord, graciously hear us.**

Father in heaven,
when the angels greeted the birth of your Son
they sang for joy 'Glory to God and peace on earth'.
Bless with Christ's peace the nations of the world.

Lord, hear us.
**Lord, graciously hear us.**

Father in heaven,
your Son has promised to your children
    the care of the guardian angels who look upon your face.
Protect by your mercy our neighbours, families and friends.

Lord, hear us.
**Lord, graciously hear us.**

Father in heaven,
you give your angels charge over those who trust in you
    to guard them in all their ways.
Be with those in trouble . . .,
    rescue them and show them your salvation.

Lord, hear us.
**Lord, graciously hear us.**

Father in heaven,
your angel declares 'Blessed are the dead who die in the Lord.'
'Blessed indeed,' says the Spirit, 'for they may rest from their
    labours, for they take with them the record of their deeds.'
Enfold in your love ( . . . and) all who come in faith
    to your judgement seat in heaven.

Lord, hear us.
**Lord, graciously hear us.**

Father in heaven, the angels sing by day and night
    around your throne:
'Holy, holy, holy is the Lord God almighty.'
With Michael, prince of the angels, who contends by our side,
with Gabriel, your herald, who brings glad tidings,
and with the whole company of heaven,
we worship you, we give you glory,
**we sing your praise and exalt you for ever.   Amen.**   *9 C 1*

## *Acclamation*

The Lord commands his angels
**to keep you in all your ways.**
Give thanks to the Lord, all his angels, mighty in power,
**who fulfil his command and heed the voice of his word.**
Give thanks to the Lord, all his hosts,
**his servants that do his will.**
Give thanks to the Lord, all his works,
    in every place where he rules,
**my soul, give thanks to the Lord.**
For he commands his angels,
**to keep you in all your ways.**   *9 D 1*

## *Simple Blessing*

God keep you in the fellowship of his saints.
Christ protect you by the ministry of the angels.
The Spirit make you holy in God's service;
and the blessing . . .   *9 E 1*

## Solemn Blessing

God bring you to the home
that Christ prepares for all who love him.   **Amen.**

God give you the will to live each day
in life eternal.   **Amen.**

God grant you the citizenship of heaven,
with his blessed and beloved,
and the whole company of the redeemed.   **Amen.**

And the blessing . . .                                    *9 F 1*


## THE EUCHARIST

## Introduction to the Peace

Hear again the song of the angels:
Glory to God in the highest, and on earth peace.         *9 G 1*


## Eucharistic Preface

1    Through him the archangels sing your praise,
     the angels fulfil your commands,
     the cherubim and seraphim continually proclaim your holiness;
     the whole company of heaven glorifies your name
         and rejoices to do your will.
     Therefore we pray that our voices may be heard with theirs,
     for ever praising you and saying
     **Holy, holy, holy, Lord . . .**                    *9 H 1*

2    And now we give you thanks and praise your holy name
     because the splendour of your faithful angels and archangels
         shows us your greatness,
     which surpasses in goodness the whole of creation.
     So as the hosts of angels rejoice in your glory,
     we give you, their Creator, glory and worship.

In adoration and joy we make their hymn of praise our own:
**Holy, holy, holy Lord . . .**                                    *9 H 2*

## Words at the Breaking of Bread

God rains down manna for us to eat
and gives us the grain of heaven.
**So on earth
we share the bread of angels.**                                    *9 J 1*

## Invitation to Communion

I heard the voice of a great multitude crying, Alleluia!
    The Lord our God has entered into his kingdom.
**Blessed are those who are called
    to the supper of the Lamb. Alleluia!**                         *9 K 1*

## Prayers after Communion

1   Lord of heaven,
    in this eucharist you have brought us near
        to an innumerable company of angels
        and to the spirits of the saints made perfect.
    As in this food of our earthly pilgrimage
        we have shared their fellowship,
    so may we come to share their joy in heaven;
    through Jesus Christ our Lord.   **Amen.**                     *9 L 1*

2   Eternal God,
    you have fed us with the bread of angels.
    May we who come under their protection,
    like them give you continual service and praise;
    through Jesus Christ our Lord.   **Amen.**                     *9 L 2*

## DAILY PRAYER

# *Light Prayer*

Blessed are you, Sovereign God, Lord of hosts,
hidden in the mystery of light,
ceaselessly adored by countless holy angels.
At creation the holy ones sang for joy;
the universe is filled with the messengers of your glory.
The mysterious powers marvelled
   to see you create a new people.
The rebellious powers could not penetrate
   the secret wisdom of Calvary.
The fearsome enemies of life were disarmed
   and led captive at the cross.
The hosts in glory watched
   the world's deceiver fall from heaven.
With joy the angels welcome each returning sinner
   and guard the path of all who trust in you.
Awesome in judgement, unlimited in mercy,
blessed are you, Sovereign God, enthroned in light.
**Amen.**                                    *9 M 1*

# *Canticle*

1    Te Deum 1–13 (ASB page 55)

2    Bless the Lord (ASB page 65)

# *Pattern of Readings with Psalms and Canticles*

1    Exodus 23.20–23
       Psalm 91.1–11

2    Job 28.1–7
       Psalm 8

3    Daniel 12.1–4
       Psalm 104.1–5,32–35

4    Acts 12.1–11
       Psalm 34.1–8

5    Revelation 1.1–5
       Psalm 148.1–6

6    Revelation 14.14–18
       Canticle: Great and Wonderful (ASB page 54)

Gospel   Matthew 18.1–6,10            *9 P 1*

# Ending

Blessing and honour and thanksgiving and praise
more than we can utter, more than we can conceive,
be to you, most holy and glorious Trinity,
Father, Son, and Holy Spirit,
by all angels, all people, all creatures,
for ever and ever.  **Amen.**        *9 Q 1*

# 10   DEDICATION

The Dedication Festival of a church is kept either on or near the day
of its dedication, when this is known, or else in October. A long
tradition assigns it to the first Sunday in October. *The Promise of His
Glory* suggests the last Sunday in October.

'Dedication' is a frequent theme in Christian worship. In a sense
every act of worship is a moment of dedication for the worshippers.
The particular significance of this festival is to celebrate the part that
the church building can play in the life, worship and mission of a
Christian community.

## Invitation to Confession

> We are a temple of God's indwelling Holy Spirit,
>     yet we have grieved him.
> The temple of our bodies does not belong to us,
> but was bought with the price of Christ's precious blood.
> So we come, in sorrow yet with confidence,
> to ask forgiveness of our Father in heaven.          *10 A 1*

## Penitential Kyrie

> Zeal for your house has eaten me up:
> and the taunts of those who taunt you have fallen on me.
> Lord, have mercy.
> **Lord, have mercy.**
>
> I would rather stand at the threshold of the house of my God:
> than dwell in the tents of ungodliness.
> Christ, have mercy.
> **Christ, have mercy.**

The Lord will defend your going out and your coming in:
from this time forward for evermore.
Lord, have mercy.
**Lord, have mercy.**                                      *10 B 1*

## *Intercession*

For the Church universal, of which these buildings are a visible
symbol,
**Lord, receive our thanks and prayer.**

For this congregation as we remember your promise that when
two or three are gathered in your name you are there in the
midst of them,
**Lord, receive our thanks and prayer.**

For this place where we may be still and know that you are God,
**Lord, receive our thanks and prayer.**

For the fulfilling of our desires and petitions as you see best for
us,
**Lord, receive our thanks and prayer.**

For your blessings in the past and for a vision of the future,
**Lord, receive our thanks and prayer.**

For the gift of the Holy Spirit and new life in baptism,
**Lord, receive our thanks and prayer.**

For the pardon of our sins when we fall short of your glory,
**Lord, receive our thanks and prayer.**

For a foretaste of your eternal kingdom in the sacrament of the
eucharist,
**Lord, receive our thanks and prayer.**

For the blessing of our vows and the crowning of our years
with your goodness,
**Lord, receive our thanks and prayer.**

For the faith of those who have gone before us and for grace to persevere like them,
**Lord, receive our thanks and prayer.**

For all the benefactors of this place who have died in the peace of Christ and are at rest,
**Lord, receive our thanks and prayer.**

For a sense of our fellowship with (N our patron and) all your saints,
**Lord, receive our thanks and prayer.**

O God, from living and chosen stones
   you prepare an everlasting dwelling-place for your majesty.
Grant that in the power of the Holy Spirit
   those who serve you here
   may always be kept within your presence.
This we pray through Jesus Christ our Lord.   **Amen.**   *10 C 1*


## Acclamation

How awesome is this place!
**This is none other than the house of God,**
**and this is the gateway of heaven!**

I saw a ladder which rested on the ground
with its top reaching to heaven
and the angels of God were going up and down it.
**This is none other than the house of God,**
**and this is the gateway of heaven!**

You will see greater things than this.
You will see heaven wide open,
and God's angels ascending and descending upon the Son of
   Man.
**This is none other than the house of God,**
**and this is the gateway of heaven!**

You are the temple of the living God,
and the Spirit of God dwells in you.
The temple of God is holy, and you are that temple.
**This is none other than the house of God,
and this is the gateway of heaven!**                    *10 D 1*

## Simple Blessing

Christ, whose glory is in the heavens,
fill this house and illuminate your hearts;
and the blessing . . .                    *10 E 1*

## Solemn Blessing

God bring you to the home
that Christ prepares for all who love him.   **Amen.**

God give you the will to live each day
in life eternal.   **Amen.**

God grant you the citizenship of heaven,
with his blessed and beloved,
and the whole company of the redeemed.   **Amen.**

And the blessing . . .                    *10 F 1*

## THE EUCHARIST

## Introduction to the Peace

Peace to this house from God our heavenly Father.
Peace to this house from his Son who is our peace.
Peace to this house from the Holy Spirit the Life-giver.

And the peace of the Lord be always with you
**and also with you.**                    *10 G 1*

## Eucharistic Preface

1 And now we give you thanks
for your blessing on this house of prayer,
where through your grace we offer you the sacrifice of praise,
and are built by your Spirit
into a temple made without hands,
even the body of your Son Jesus Christ.
Therefore . . .                                                    *10 H 1*

2 And now we give you thanks that,
though the heaven of heavens cannot contain you,
and your glory is in all the world,
yet you choose to hallow places for your worship,
and in them you pour forth gifts of grace
    upon your faithful people.
Therefore . . .                                                    *10 H 2*

3 And now we give you thanks for this house of prayer
in which you bless your family
as we come to you on pilgrimage.
Here you reveal your presence
by sacramental signs,
and make us one with you
through the unseen bond of grace.
Here you build your temple of living stones,
and bring the Church to its full stature
as the body of Christ throughout the world,
to reach its perfection at last
in the heavenly city of Jerusalem,
which is the vision of your peace.
Therefore . . .                                                    *10 H 3*

## Words at the Breaking of Bread

We break this bread
to share in the body of Christ.
**Though we are many, we are one body,**
**because we all share in one bread.**                             *10 J 1*

## *Invitation to Communion*

The gifts of God for the people of God.
**Jesus Christ is holy,**
**Jesus Christ is Lord,**
**to the glory of God the Father.**                    *10 K 1*


## *Prayers after Communion*

1   Bring us, O Lord, at our last awakening
    into the house and gate of heaven,
    to enter into that gate and dwell in that house
    where shall be no darkness nor dazzling,
       but one equal light;
    no noise nor silence, but one equal music;
    no fears nor hopes, but one equal possession;
    no ends nor beginnings, but one equal eternity
    in the habitations of your glory and dominion,
    world without end.   **Amen.**                    *10 L 1*

2   Father,
    you make your Church on earth
    a sign of the new and eternal Jerusalem.
    By sharing in this sacrament
    may we become the temple of your presence
    and the home of your glory;
    through Jesus Christ our Lord.   **Amen.**                    *10 L 2*

3   God our Father,
    in this house of prayer
       you bless your family on its earthly pilgrimage:
    so quicken our consciences by your holiness,
    nourish our minds by your truth,
    purify our imaginations by your beauty,
    and open our hearts to your love,
    that, in the surrender of our wills to your purpose,
    the world may be renewed
       in Jesus Christ our Lord.   **Amen.**                    *10 L 3*

DAILY PRAYER

## Light Prayer

Blessed are you, Sovereign God, Saviour of all.
You give light to those who walk in darkness,
and desire that in every place
> prayer shall be offered in Jesus' name.
We bless you for grace made known in this house of prayer,
> for the gathering of your people,
> for sins forgiven, for lives made new,
> for light that shines from the Scriptures,
> for love made known at your table,
> for the foretaste of heaven in (N and) all your saints.
Hope of the nations, refuge of the weary,
Blessed are you, Sovereign God, Light of the World.
**Amen.**

*10 M 1*

## Canticle

### A SONG OF THE HOLY CITY

[Response **Behold, I make all things new.**]

1    Then I saw a new heaven and a new earth:
for the first heaven and the first earth
> had passed away
> and the sea was no more.

2    And I saw the holy city, new Jerusalem
> coming down out of heaven from God:
prepared as a bride adorned for her husband.   **[R]**

3    And I heard a great voice from the throne saying:
'Behold, the dwelling of God is with his people.

4    He will dwell with them and they shall be his own:
and God himself will be with them.   **[R]**

5    He will wipe away every tear from their eyes:
and death shall be no more.

6    Neither shall there be mourning
    nor crying nor pain any more:
for the former things have passed away.'

7    And he who sat upon the throne said:
'Behold I make all things new.'  **[R]**              *10 N 1*

## Pattern of Readings with Psalms and Canticles

1    1 Chronicles 29.6–19
    Psalm 122

2    1 Kings 8.54–62
    Psalm 46

3    2 Chronicles 7.1–11
    A Song of the New Jerusalem (*The Promise* page 311)

4    1 Maccabees 4.36–37,52–59
    Psalm 118.19–end

5    Hebrews 10.19–25
    Psalm 48.8–end

6    Ephesians 2.8–end
    A Canticle of the Holy City (*10 N 1* above)

Gospel   John 10.22–end             *10 P 1*

## Ending

God bless this church and parish,
and prosper all our attempts to be faithful
and to draw others to him,
for Jesus Christ's sake.  **Amen.**          *10 Q 1*

# EUCHARISTIC PRAYERS
# FROM HOLY COMMUNION RITE A

*First Eucharistic Prayer*

President The Lord be with you *or* The Lord is here.
**All** **and also with you.** **His Spirit is with us.**

President Lift up your hearts.
**All** **We lift them to the Lord.**

President Let us give thanks to the Lord our God.
**All** **It is right to give him thanks and praise.**

President It is indeed right,
it is our duty and our joy,
at all times and in all places
to give you thanks and praise,
holy Father, heavenly King,
almighty and eternal God,
through Jesus Christ your only Son our Lord.

For he is your living Word;
through him you have created all things from
the beginning,
and formed us in your own image.

Through him you have freed us from the
slavery of sin,
giving him to be born as man and to die upon
the cross;
you raised him from the dead
and exalted him to your right hand on high.

Through him you have sent upon us
your holy and life-giving Spirit,
and made us a people for your own possession.

[PROPER PREFACE]

Therefore with angels and archangels,
and with all the company of heaven,
we proclaim your great and glorious name,
for ever praising you and saying:

**All**    **Holy, holy, holy Lord,**
**God of power and might,**
**heaven and earth are full of your glory.**
**Hosanna in the highest.**

This ANTHEM may also be used.

**Blessed is he who comes in the name of**
   **the Lord.**
**Hosanna in the highest.**

President    Accept our praises, heavenly Father,
through your Son our Saviour Jesus Christ;
and as we follow his example and obey
   his command,
grant that by the power of your Holy Spirit
these gifts of bread and wine
may be to us his body and his blood;

Who in the same night that he was betrayed,
took bread and gave you thanks;
he broke it and gave it to his disciples, saying,
Take, eat; this is my body which is given for you;
do this in remembrance of me.
In the same way, after supper
he took the cup and gave you thanks;
he gave it to them, saying,
Drink this, all of you;
this is my blood of the new covenant,
which is shed for you and for many for the
   forgiveness of sins.
Do this, as often as you drink it,
in remembrance of me.

**All**    ★ **Christ has died:**
**Christ is risen:**
**Christ will come again.**

101

President    Therefore, heavenly Father,
we remember his offering of himself
made once for all upon the cross,
and proclaim his mighty resurrection and
   glorious ascension.
As we look for his coming in glory,
we celebrate with this bread and this cup
his one perfect sacrifice.

Accept through him, our great high priest,
this our sacrifice of thanks and praise;
and as we eat and drink these holy gifts
in the presence of your divine majesty,
renew us by your Spirit,
inspire us with your love,
and unite us in the body of your Son,
Jesus Christ our Lord.

Through him, and with him, and in him,
by the power of the Holy Spirit,
with all who stand before you in earth
   and heaven,
we worship you, Father almighty,
in songs of everlasting praise:

---

* Alternative Acclamations

**Dying you destroyed our death,
rising you restored our life.
Lord Jesus, come in glory.**

**When we eat this bread and drink this cup,
we proclaim your death, Lord Jesus,
until you come in glory.**

**Lord, by your cross and resurrection
you have set us free.
You are the Saviour of the world.**

All        **Blessing and honour and glory and power
be yours for ever and ever.   Amen.**

Silence may be kept.


## *Second Eucharistic Prayer*

President    The Lord be with you *or* The Lord is here.
All          **and also with you.       His Spirit is with us.**

President    Lift up your hearts.
All          **We lift them to the Lord.**

President    Let us give thanks to the Lord our God.
All          **It is right to give him thanks and praise.**

President    It is indeed right,
             it is our duty and our joy,
             at all times and in all places
             to give you thanks and praise,
             holy Father, heavenly King,
             almighty and eternal God,
             through Jesus Christ your only Son our Lord.

The following may be omitted if a Proper Preface is used.

             For he is your living Word;
             through him you have created all things from
                 the beginning,
             and formed us in your own image.

             Through him you have freed us from the
                 slavery of sin,
             giving him to be born as man and to die upon
                 the cross;
             you raised him from the dead
             and exalted him to your right hand on high.

             Through him you have sent upon us
             your holy and life-giving Spirit,
             and made us a people for your own possession.

[PROPER PREFACE]

Therefore with angels and archangels,
and with all the company of heaven,
we proclaim your great and glorious name,
for ever praising you and saying:

**All**　　**Holy, holy, holy Lord,**
**God of power and might,**
**heaven and earth are full of your glory.**
**Hosanna in the highest.**

This ANTHEM may also be used.

**Blessed is he who comes in the name of**
**the Lord.**
**Hosanna in the highest.**

President　Hear us, heavenly Father,
through Jesus Christ your Son our Lord,
through him accept our sacrifice of praise;
and grant that by the power of your Holy Spirit
these gifts of bread and wine
may be to us his body and his blood;

Who in the same night that he was betrayed,
took bread and gave you thanks;
he broke it and gave it to his disciples, saying,
Take, eat; this is my body which is given for you;
do this in remembrance of me.
In the same way, after supper
he took the cup and gave you thanks;
he gave it to them, saying,
Drink this, all of you;
this is my blood of the new covenant,
which is shed for you and for many for the
forgiveness of sins.
Do this, as often as you drink it,
in remembrance of me.

**All**    ★ **Christ has died:**
**Christ is risen:**
**Christ will come again.**

President   Therefore, Lord and heavenly Father,
having in remembrance his death once for all
   upon the cross,
his resurrection from the dead,
and his ascension into heaven,
and looking for the coming of his kingdom,
we make with this bread and this cup
the memorial of Christ your Son our Lord.

Accept through him this offering of our duty
   and service;
and as we eat and drink these holy gifts
in the presence of your divine majesty,
fill us with your grace and heavenly blessing;
nourish us with the body and blood of your Son,
that we may grow into his likeness
and, made one by your Spirit,
become a living temple to your glory.

---

★ Alternative Acclamations

**Dying you destroyed our death,**
**rising you restored our life.**
**Lord Jesus, come in glory.**

**When we eat this bread and drink this cup,**
**we proclaim your death, Lord Jesus,**
**until you come in glory.**

**Lord, by your cross and resurrection**
**you have set us free.**
**You are the Saviour of the world.**

Through Jesus Christ our Lord,
by whom, and with whom, and in whom,
in the unity of the Holy Spirit,
all honour and glory be yours, almighty Father,
from all who stand before you in earth
   and heaven,
now and for ever. **Amen.**

Silence may be kept.

## Third Eucharistic Prayer

President  The Lord be with you *or* The Lord is here.
**All**      **and also with you.**     **His Spirit is with us.**

President  Lift up your hearts.
**All**      **We lift them to the Lord.**

President  Let us give thanks to the Lord our God.
**All**      **It is right to give him thanks and praise.**

President  Father, we give you thanks and praise
through your beloved Son Jesus Christ,
your living Word through whom you have
   created all things;

Who was sent by you, in your great goodness,
   to be our Saviour;
by the power of the Holy Spirit he took flesh
and, as your Son, born of the blessed Virgin,
was seen on earth
and went about among us;

He opened wide his arms for us on the cross;
he put an end to death by dying for us
and revealed the resurrection by rising to
   new life;
so he fulfilled your will and won for you a
   holy people.

[PROPER PREFACE]

Therefore with angels and archangels,
and with all the company of heaven,
we proclaim your great and glorious name,
for ever praising you and saying:

**All**      **Holy, holy, holy Lord,**
**God of power and might,**
**heaven and earth are full of your glory.**
**Hosanna in the highest.**

This ANTHEM may also be used.

**Blessed is he who comes in the name of**
   **the Lord.**
**Hosanna in the highest.**

President   Lord, you are holy indeed, the source of
   all holiness;
grant that, by the power of your Holy Spirit,
and according to your holy will,
these your gifts of bread and wine
may be to us the body and blood of our Lord
   Jesus Christ;

Who in the same night that he was betrayed,
took bread and gave you thanks;
he broke it and gave it to his disciples, saying,
Take, eat; this is my body which is given for you;
do this in remembrance of me.
In the same way, after supper
he took the cup and gave you thanks;
he gave it to them, saying,
Drink this, all of you;
this is my blood of the new covenant,
which is shed for you and for many for the
   forgiveness of sins.
Do this, as often as you drink it,
in remembrance of me.

**All**    \* **Christ has died:**
**Christ is risen:**
**Christ will come again.**

President    And so, Father, calling to mind his death on
the cross,
his perfect sacrifice made once for the sins
of all,
rejoicing at his mighty resurrection and
~~glorious ascension,~~
and looking for his coming in glory,
we celebrate this memorial of our redemption;
we thank you for counting us worthy
go stand in your presence and serve you;
we bring before you this bread and this cup;

We pray you to accept this our duty and service,
a spiritual sacrifice of praise and thanksgiving;

Send the Holy Spirit on your people
and gather into one in your kingdom
all who share this one bread and one cup,

---

\* Alternative Acclamations

**Dying you destroyed our death,**
**rising you restored our life.**
**Lord Jesus, come in glory.**

**When we eat this bread and drink this cup,**
**we proclaim your death, Lord Jesus,**
**until you come in glory.**

**Lord, by your cross and resurrection**
**you have set us free.**
**You are the Saviour of the world.**

so that we, in the company of all the saints,
may praise and glorify you for ever,
through him from whom all good things come,
Jesus Christ our Lord;

By whom, and with whom, and in whom,
in the unity of the Holy Spirit,
all honour and glory be yours, almighty Father,
for ever and ever. **Amen.**

Silence may be kept.

## Fourth Eucharistic Prayer

President   The Lord be with you *or* The Lord is here.
**All**     **and also with you.     His Spirit is with us.**

President   Lift up your hearts.
**All**     **We lift them to the Lord.**

President   Let us give thanks to the Lord our God.
**All**     **It is right to give him thanks and praise.**

President   It is indeed right,
it is our duty and our joy,
at all times and in all places
to give you thanks and praise,
holy Father, heavenly King,
almighty and eternal God,
creator of heaven and earth,
through Jesus Christ our Lord:

[PROPER PREFACE]

Therefore with angels and archangels,
and with all the company of heaven,
we proclaim your great and glorious name,
for ever praising you and saying:

**All**     **Holy, holy, holy Lord,**
**God of power and might,**
**heaven and earth are full of your glory.**
**Hosanna in the highest.**

This ANTHEM may also be used.

**Blessed is he who comes in the name of**
**the Lord.**
**Hosanna in the highest.**

President     All glory to you, our heavenly Father:
in your tender mercy
you gave your only Son Jesus Christ
to suffer death upon the cross for
  our redemption;
he made there
a full atonement for the sins of the whole world,
offering once for all his one sacrifice of himself;
he instituted,
and in his holy gospel commanded us
  to continue,
a perpetual memory of his precious death
until he comes again.

Hear us, merciful Father, we humbly pray,
and grant that by the power of your Holy Spirit
we who receive these gifts of your creation,
this bread and this wine,
according to your Son our Saviour Jesus Christ's
  holy institution,
in remembrance of the death that he suffered,
may be partakers of his most blessed body
  and blood;

Who in the same night that he was betrayed,
took bread and gave you thanks;
he broke it and gave it to his disciples, saying,
Take, eat; this is my body which is given for you;
do this in remembrance of me.

In the same way, after supper
he took the cup and gave you thanks;
he gave it to them, saying,

Drink this, all of you;
this is my blood of the new covenant,
which is shed for you and for many for the
    forgiveness of sins.
Do this, as often as you drink it,
in remembrance of me.

**All**     * **Christ has died:**
            **Christ has risen:**
            **Christ will come again.**

President   Therefore, Lord and heavenly Father,
            in remembrance of the precious death
                and passion,
            the mighty resurrection and glorious ascension
            of your dear Son Jesus Christ,
            we offer you through him this sacrifice of
                praise and thanksgiving.

---

* Alternative Acclamations

**Dying you destroyed our death,**
**rising you restored our life.**
**Lord Jesus, come in glory.**

**When we eat this bread and drink this cup,**
**we proclaim your death, Lord Jesus,**
**until you come in glory.**

**Lord, by your cross and resurrection**
**you have set us free.**
**You are the Saviour of the world.**

Grant that by his merits and death,
and through faith in his blood,
we and all your Church may receive forgiveness
 of our sins
and all other benefits of his passion.
Although we are unworthy, through our
 many sins,
to offer you any sacrifice,
yet we pray that you will accept this,
the duty and service that we owe;
do not weigh our merits, but pardon
 our offences,
and fill us all who share in this
 holy communion
with your grace and heavenly blessing.

Through Jesus Christ our Lord,
by whom, and with whom, and in whom,
in the unity of the Holy Spirit,
all honour and glory be yours, almighty Father,
now and for ever. **Amen.**

Silence may be kept.

# TEXTS BEFORE THE DISTRIBUTION FROM HOLY COMMUNION RITE A

*The Lord's Prayer*

As our Saviour taught us, so we pray.
**Our Father in heaven,**
**hallowed be your name,**
**your kingdom come,**
**your will be done,**
**on earth as in heaven.**
**Give us today our daily bread.**
**Forgive us our sins**
**as we forgive those who sin against us.**
**Lead us not into temptation**
**but deliver us from evil.**

**For the kingdom, the power, and the glory**
**are yours**
**now and for ever.   Amen.**

**Our Father, who art in heaven,**
**hallowed be thy name;**
**thy kingdom come;**
**thy will be done;**
**on earth as it is in heaven.**
**Give us this day our daily bread.**
**And forgive us our trespasses,**
**as we forgive those who trespass**
**against us.**
**And lead us not into temptation;**
**but deliver us from evil.**

**For thine is the kingdom, the power,**
**and the glory,**
**for ever and ever.   Amen.**

## At the Breaking of the Bread

We break this bread
to share in the body of Christ.
**Though we are many, we are one body,
because we all share in one bread.**

**Lamb of God, you take away the sins of
the world:
have mercy on us.**

**Lamb of God, you take away the sins of
the world:
have mercy on us.**

**Lamb of God, you take away the sins of
the world:
grant us peace.**

or  **Jesus, Lamb of God: have mercy on us.
Jesus, bearer of our sins: have mercy on us.
Jesus, redeemer of the world: give us
your peace.**

## Immediately Before the Distribution

Draw near with faith. Receive the body of our
Lord Jesus Christ which he gave for you, and his
blood which he shed for you.

Eat and drink in remembrance that he died for
you, and feed on him in your hearts by faith with
thanksgiving.

# 11 THE BLESSED VIRGIN MARY

## Invitation to Confession

We have done what was wrong in the Lord's sight
and chosen what displeased him.
Yet as a mother comforts her child,
so shall the Lord himself comfort us.
So let us come to him who knows our every deed and
    thought.                                                     *11 A 1*

## Penitential Kyrie

Lord Jesus, you are mighty God and Prince of Peace:
Lord, have mercy.
**Lord, have mercy.**

Lord Jesus, you are Son of God and Son of Mary:
Christ, have mercy.
**Christ, have mercy.**

Lord Jesus, you are Word made flesh
    and splendour of the Father:
Lord, have mercy.
**Lord, have mercy.**                                            *11 B 1*

## Intercession

As we pray to God, the Father of our Lord Jesus Christ, we say
with Mary:
Lord, have mercy on those who fear you.
**Holy is your name.**

Your prophet of old foretold a day when a virgin would
conceive and bear a son who would be called God-with-us.
Help us to look forward to your deliverance and to seek the
fulness of your kingdom.

Lord, have mercy on those who fear you.
**Holy is your name.**

Your angel declared to Mary that she was to be the mother of the Saviour. Help ( . . . and) every Christian person to be open to your word and obedient to your will.

Lord, have mercy on those who fear you.
**Holy is your name.**

Mary rejoiced with Elizabeth, and sang your praise, 'My soul proclaims the greatness of the Lord.' Help us to live joyful lives that sing your praise.

Lord, have mercy on those who fear you.
**Holy is your name.**

Mary bore a son of David's line, born a king whose reign would never end. Bless ( . . . and) all the nations of the world with Christ's gift of peace.

Lord, have mercy on those who fear you.
**Holy is your name.**

The child Jesus grew in wisdom and stature in the home of Mary and Joseph. Strengthen our homes and families, and keep under your protection ( . . . and) all those whom we love.

Lord, have mercy on those who fear you.
**Holy is your name.**

At the foot of the cross of Christ stood his mother, and from the cross she received his lifeless body in her arms. Give comfort and healing to ( . . . and) all who suffer and all who watch the suffering of those they love.

Lord, have mercy on those who fear you.
**Holy is your name.**

The apostle John saw a vision of a woman in heaven, robed
with the sun. Bring us with ( . . . and) all those who have died
in the faith of Christ to share the joy of heaven with Mary and
all the saints.

Lord, have mercy on those who fear you.
**Holy is your name.**

Almighty and everlasting God,
you have stooped to raise fallen humanity
by the child-bearing of blessed Mary;
grant that we who have seen your glory
revealed in our human nature,
and your love made perfect in our weakness,
may daily be renewed in your image,
and conformed to the pattern of your Son,
Jesus Christ our Lord.  **Amen.**                    11 C 1

## Acclamation

Blessed is she who has had faith
that the Lord's promise would be fulfilled.
**All generations shall call her blessed.**
So tenderly has he looked upon his servant.
**All generations shall call her blessed.**
Blessed is she among women and
   blessed is the fruit of her womb.
**All generations shall call her blessed.**
Glory to the Father, and to the Son, and to the Holy Spirit.
**Holy is his name.**                              11 D 1

## Simple Blessing

Christ the Son of God, born of Mary,
fill you with his grace to trust his promises
and obey his will;
and the blessing . . .                             11 E 1

## Solemn Blessing

May the Father,
who has loved the eternal Son
from before the foundation of the world,
shed that love upon you his children. **Amen.**

May Christ,
who by his incarnation gathered into one
things earthly and heavenly,
fill you with joy and peace. **Amen.**

May the Holy Spirit,
by whose overshadowing Mary became the God-bearer,
give you grace to carry the good news of Christ. **Amen.**

And the blessing . . . *11 F 1*


## THE EUCHARIST

## Introduction to the Peace

Unto us a child is born, unto us a son is given:
and his name is called the Prince of Peace. *11 G 1*


## Eucharistic Preface

1    And now we give you thanks
because in choosing the blessed Virgin Mary
   to be the mother of your Son
   you have exalted the humble and meek.
Your angel hailed her as most highly favoured;
with all generations we call her blessed,
and with her we rejoice and magnify your holy name.
Therefore . . . *11 H 1*

2　And now we give you thanks
because by the power of the Holy Spirit
he took our nature upon him
and was born of the Virgin Mary his mother,
that being himself without sin
he might make us clean from all sin.
Therefore . . .　　　　　　　　　　　　　　　　　*11 H 2*

3　And now we give you thanks
that he is your eternal Son, the King of glory.
When he took our flesh to set us free
he did not abhor the Virgin's womb.
Seated at your right hand in glory,
he will come to be our judge
and to bring us with the saints to glory everlasting.
Therefore . . .　　　　　　　　　　　　　　　　　*11 H 3*

See also *2 H 1* and *2 H 2*.


## Words at the Breaking of Bread

We break the bread of life,
and that life is the Light of the world.
**God here among us,**
**light in the midst of us,**
**bring us to light and life.**　　　　　　　　　　*11 J 1*


## Invitation to Communion

I heard the voice of a great multitude crying, Alleluia!
　The Lord our God has entered into his kingdom.
**Blessed are those who are called**
　**to the supper of the Lamb. Alleluia!**　　　　*11 K 1*

## *Prayers after Communion*

1   Almighty God,
     your word proclaims our salvation;
     your table gives us life.
     Grant us the humble obedience we see in Mary,
     that we too may respond as willing servants.
     We ask this in the name of Jesus Christ our Lord.   **Amen.**

*11 L 1*

2   O Lord,
     your handmaid bore the Word
     made flesh for our redemption.
     Help us by this sacrament
     to make known your love in all the world;
     through Jesus Christ our Lord.   **Amen.**          *11 L 2*


DAILY PRAYER

## *Light Prayer*

Blessed are you, Lord our God, King of the universe:
to you be glory and praise for ever!
In the greatness of your mercy you chose the Virgin Mary
to be the mother of your only Son.
In her obedience the day of our redemption dawned
when by the overshadowing of your Holy Spirit
he took our flesh and dwelt in the darkness of her womb.
In her your glory shines as in the burning bush,
and so we call her blessed with every generation.
With her we rejoice in your salvation
and ponder in our hearts the mystery of your love.
May we bear with her the piercing sword of sorrow
in hope that we like her may share the joy of heaven,
as now we join our praise with hers, blessed among all women,
create in us a heart of love obedient to your will,
for you are Lord and you are our God for ever.   **Amen.**   *11 M 1*

# *Canticles*

## 1 THE SONG OF HANNAH

[Response **The Lord has filled my heart with joy.**]

1   My heart exults in the Lord:
    I find my strength in my God.

2   My mouth laughs at my enemies:
    as I rejoice at your saving help.   **[R]**

3   The bows of the mighty are broken:
    but the feeble are clothed with strength.

4   Those with plenty must labour for bread:
    but the hungry are hungry no more.

5   The barren woman has children now:
    but the fruitful wife is left forlorn.   **[R]**

6   It is the Lord who gives life and death:
    he sends down to the grave and raises up.

7   It is the Lord who gives poverty and wealth:
    he humbles some and makes others great.   **[R]**

8   The Lord lifts up the weak from the dust:
    and raises the poor from their misery.

9   He makes them companions of princes:
    and sets them on thrones of honour.

10  For the foundations of the earth are the Lord's:
    on them he has built the world.   **[R]**   *11 N 1*

## 2 A SONG OF THE BRIDE

[Response **The Lord has clothed me
with the garments of salvation.**]

1   I will greatly rejoice in the Lord:
    my soul shall exult in my God,

2   For he has clothed me with the garments of salvation:
he has covered me with the cloak of integrity.

3   As a bridegroom decks himself with a garland:
and as a bride adorns herself with her jewels.  **[R]**

4   For as the earth puts forth her blossom:
and as seeds in the garden spring up,

5   So shall the Lord God make righteousness and praise:
blossom before all the nations.  **[R]**

6   For Zion's sake, I will not keep silence:
and for Jerusalem's sake, I will not rest.

7   Until her deliverance shines forth as the sunrise:
and her salvation as a burning torch.  **[R]**

8   The nations shall see your deliverance:
and all kings shall see your glory.

9   Then you shall be called by a new name:
which the mouth of the Lord will give.

10  You shall be a crown of glory in the hand of the Lord:
and a royal diadem in the hand of your God.  **[R]**      *11 N 2*


## 3 A SONG OF JUDITH

[Response **Blessed are you by God most high.**]

1   Blessed be the Lord our God:
who has created the heavens and the earth.

2   And blessed be you, my daughter, by God Most High:
beyond all women on earth.  **[R]**

3   The trust you have shown shall not pass from human hearts:
it will ever remind us of the power of God.

4   You have walked in the straight path before our God:
you have done great good to Israel.

5   You are the exaltation of Jerusalem, the glory of Israel:
    may the almighty Lord bless you for ever.   **[R]**          *11 N 3*

## *Patterns of Readings with Psalms and Canticles*

## *1   Theme: The Annunciation*

1   Genesis 3.(1–7)8–15
    Psalm 8

2   2 Samuel 7.4,8–16
    Psalm 132.1–13

3   Isaiah 61.10—62.3
    Psalm 87

4   Proverbs 8.22–31
    Psalm 138

5   Wisdom 9.1–12
    Psalm 2 or 110

6   Galatians 4.1–5 or
    Romans 5.12–end
    Magnificat

Gospel   Matthew 1.18–23                                          *11 P 1*

## *2   Theme: The Feast of the Blessed Virgin Mary*

1   1 Chronicles 15.3–4,15–16; 16.1–2
    Psalm 132.1–9,13–14

2   Isaiah 61.10—62.3
    Psalm 113

3   Jeremiah 31.1–14
    Canticle: A Song of Judith (*11 N 3* above)

4   Ecclesiasticus 24.17–end
    Psalm 45.1–2,9–end

123

5     Acts 1.6–14
        Psalm 115.8–end

6     1 Corinthians 15.54–57
        Canticle: A Song of the Holy City (*The Promise* page 332)

Gospel   Luke 11.27–28                                        *11 P 2*


## Ending

May the love of the Holy Family surround you.
May the joy that was Mary's refresh you.
May the faithfulness that was Joseph's encourage you.
May the peace of the Christ Child fill your lives.   **Amen.**

*11 Q 1*

# 12 APOSTLES AND EVANGELISTS

Much of this material is suitable for use on any saint's day, though some is specific to apostles and evangelists. Some of it has the sort of festal or solemn tone that would be more appropriate for a special parish celebration, such as a patronal festival, than for an ordinary weekday said celebration.

Some of the material in Chapter 13 is also suitable for use on the festivals of apostles and evangelists.

## Invitation to Confession

1   We run the race set before us,
    surrounded by a great cloud of witnesses.
    Therefore let us lay aside every weight,
    and the sin which clings so closely,
    bringing them to Jesus in penitence and faith.                12 A 1

2   Jesus said to his apostles,
    'You are my friends if you obey my commands.'
    Let us now confess our disobedience to him.                   12 A 2

## Penitential Kyrie

1   You were sent to preach the good news of light
        in the darkness of the world:
    Lord, have mercy.
    **Lord, have mercy.**

    You were sent to plant in our hearts the seed of eternal life:
    Christ, have mercy.
    **Christ, have mercy.**

    You were sent to reconcile us to yourself
        by the shedding of your blood:
    Lord, have mercy.
    **Lord, have mercy.**                                         12 B 1

2    Lord Jesus, in your love you invite us to be your friends:
     Lord, have mercy.
     **Lord, have mercy.**

     Lord Jesus, in your joy you choose us to go out and bear fruit:
     Christ, have mercy.
     **Christ, have mercy.**

     Lord Jesus, in your power you send us to be your faithful
        witnesses:
     Lord, have mercy.
     **Lord, have mercy.**                                    *12 B 2*


## Intercession

1    Encouraged by our fellowship with all the saints,
     let us make our prayers to the Father through our Lord Jesus
     Christ.

     Father, your Son called men and women to leave the past
     behind them and to follow him as his disciples in the way of
     the cross. Look with mercy upon those whom he has called
     today, marked with the cross and made his disciples within the
     Church . . .

     Lord, have mercy.
     **Christ, have mercy.**

     Your Son told his disciples not to be afraid, and at Easter
     breathed on them his gift of peace. Look with mercy upon the
     world into which he sent them out, and give it that peace for
     which it longs . . .

     Lord, have mercy.
     **Christ, have mercy.**

     Your Son formed around him a company who were no longer
     servants but friends, and he called all those who obeyed him his
     brother and sister and mother. Look with mercy upon our
     families and our friends and upon the communities in which we
     share . . .

Lord, have mercy.
**Christ, have mercy.**

Your Son sent out disciples to preach and to heal the sick. Look
with mercy on all those who yearn to hear the good news of
salvation, and renew among your people the gifts of healing . . .

Lord, have mercy.
**Christ, have mercy.**

Your Son promised to those who followed him that they would
sit on thrones judging the twelve tribes of Israel and would
share the banquet of the kingdom. According to your promise,
look with mercy on those who have walked with Christ in this
life and now have passed through death . . .

Lord, have mercy.
**Christ, have mercy.**

Almighty God,
you have built your Church upon the foundation
  of the apostles and prophets
with Jesus Christ himself as the chief corner-stone.
So join us together in unity of spirit by their doctrine,
that we may be made an holy temple acceptable to you;
through Jesus Christ our Lord.  **Amen.**                    *12 C 1*

2   Rejoicing in the presence of the saints in heaven,
    we pray for the Church and the world, saying,
    Lord God of heaven,
    **in your mercy, hear us.**

Almighty God,
as you have surrounded your Church with a great cloud of
witnesses, give us your grace as we pray to throw off the sin
that entangles, and anything else that hinders, and to preserve
us in our pilgrimage as we hasten along the path you spread
before us.

Lord God of heaven,
**in your mercy, hear us.**

You gave your servant James the gift to lead the church at Jerusalem. You gave him the discernment to relate the words of the prophets to new growth in the Church, and to bring those of different opinions to unite in a plan which seemed good to your Holy Spirit. We pray for N our bishop and for . . . Give the leaders of your Church today discernment of your will, openness to your word and the strength of your Spirit, as they preside over the councils of the Church and plan for its growth.

Lord God of heaven,
**in your mercy, hear us.**

You gave your servant Paul wisdom to speak before kings and judges. You gave him the experience of travelling from region to region, the vision to proclaim your lordship over many countries, and the courage to declare that those from different cultures are all one in Christ Jesus. We pray for . . . Bring your world today into harmony and unity, and use the messengers of your peace to proclaim that you are Lord.

Lord God of heaven,
**in your mercy, hear us.**

You gave your servant Luke skill as a doctor, a sympathetic understanding of the down-trodden, and loyalty to his friends in difficulties and in prison . . . We pray for those today who need healing, understanding, support and friendship, especially . . .

Lord God of heaven,
**in your mercy, hear us.**

You gave your servant N . . .
We pray for . . .

Lord God of heaven,
**in your mercy, hear us.**

You gave your servant Stephen a sight of heaven as he died, and Jesus standing at your right hand; and even as he died you kept him in conversation with you as he thought of others and prayed, 'Lord Jesus, receive my spirit.' Give to those who die in faith . . . the light of an open door in heaven, the peace and assurance of speaking with Jesus, and eternal rest with all your saints in glory.

Lord God of heaven,
**in your mercy, hear us.**

Hear us in your mercy, as we fix our eyes on Jesus, author and perfecter of our faith, who for us endured the cross, and is seated at the right hand of your throne, where he intercedes for us for ever.

God our Saviour,
**you know us and love us
and hear our prayer;
keep us in the eternal fellowship
of Jesus Christ our Saviour.    Amen.**                    *12 C 2*

## Acclamation

The Lord is righteous and delights in righteous deeds;
the just shall see his face.
**The Lord is righteous and delights in righteous deeds;
the just shall see his face.**
When foundations are being destroyed,
what can the righteous do?
**The just shall see his face.**
His eyes behold the inhabited world;
his piercing eye weighs our worth.
**The just shall see his face.**
The Lord weighs the righteous as well as the wicked,
but those that delight in violence he abhors.
**The just shall see his face.**
Glory to the Father, and to the Son, and to the Holy Spirit.
**The Lord is righteous and delights in righteous deeds;
the just shall see his face.**                    *12 D 1*

## Simple Blessing

1    God give you grace to share the inheritance
      of the saints in glory;
    and the blessing . . .          *12 E 1*

2    God, who has prepared for you a city with eternal foundations,
    bring you, with all the saints,
      to the eternal and triumphant joy of that city;
    and the blessing . . .          *12 E 2*

## Solemn Blessing

God,
the Father of our Lord Jesus Christ,
give you the spirit of wisdom and revelation,
to know the hope to which he has called you.  **Amen.**

God,
who has shown you a pattern of holy living and holy dying
    in the lives of the saints,
bring you to share their glorious inheritance.  **Amen.**

God,
who calls you no longer strangers
but fellow citizens with the saints,
set your hearts and minds on things above,
where Christ is seated at God's right hand.  **Amen.**

And the blessing . . .          *12 F 1*

## THE EUCHARIST

## Introduction to the Peace

We are fellow-citizens with the saints
    and of the household of God,
through Christ our Lord
who came and preached peace to those who were far off
and those who were near.      *12 G 1*

## *Eucharistic Preface*

1   And now we give you thanks
    because your Son Jesus Christ after his resurrection
    sent forth his apostles and evangelists
    to preach the gospel to all nations
    and to teach us the way of truth.
    Therefore . . .                  *12 H 1*

2   And now we give you thanks, most gracious God,
    surrounded by a great cloud of witnesses
    and glorified in the assembly of your saints.
    The glorious company of apostles praise you.
    The noble fellowship of prophets praise you.
    The white-robed army of martyrs praise you.
    We, your holy Church, acclaim you.
    In communion with angels and archangels,
    and with all those who have served you in every age
    and worship you now in heaven,
    we raise our voice to proclaim your glory,
    for ever praising you and saying:
    **Holy, holy, holy Lord . . .**        *12 H 2*

3   And now we give you thanks
    because you founded your Church on the apostles
    to stand firm for ever,
    as the sign on earth of your infinite holiness
    and the living gospel for all to hear.
    Therefore . . .                  *12 H 3*

## *Words at the Breaking of Bread*

1   God of promise,
    you prepared a banquet for us in your kingdom.
    **Happy are those who are called
    to the supper of the Lamb!**        *12 J 1*

2     Lord, we died with you on the cross.
       **Now we are raised to new life.**
       We were buried in your tomb.
       **Now we share in your resurrection.**
       Live in us, that we may live in you.                    *12 J 2*

## Invitation to Communion

1     I heard the voice of a great multitude crying,
       Alleluia!
       The Lord our God has entered into his kingdom.
       **Blessed are those who are called
           to the supper of the Lamb.**                        *12 K 1*

The text above should not be used when 'God of promise . . .'
(*12 J 1*) has been used at the breaking of bread.

2     The gifts of God for the people of God.
       **Jesus Christ is holy,
       Jesus Christ is Lord,
       to the glory of God the Father.**                       *12 K 2*

## Prayers after Communion

1     Lord God,
       the source of truth and love,
       keep us faithful to the apostles' teaching and fellowship,
       united in prayer and the breaking of bread,
       and one in joy and simplicity of heart,
       in Jesus Christ our Lord.    **Amen.**                  *12 L 1*

2     God, the source of all holiness
       and giver of all good things:
       may we who have shared at this table
       as strangers and pilgrims here on earth
       be welcomed with all your saints

to the heavenly feast
   on the day of your kingdom;
through Jesus Christ our Lord.   **Amen.**                    *12 L 2*

3   Blessed Lord,
through whom your holy apostles fed your Church
   at the table of your word
and handed on the mysteries of Christ's body and blood:
grant that we may bring all to Christ,
   to reveal in him the gift of everlasting life;
through Jesus Christ our Lord.   **Amen.**                    *12 L 3*


DAILY PRAYER

*Light Prayer*

1   Blessed are you, Lord our God, King of the universe:
to you be glory and praise for ever!
We rejoice in the glorious splendour of your majesty.
For you have given us a share
in the inheritance of the saints in light.
In the darkness of this passing age
your saints proclaim the glory of your kingdom.
Chosen as lights in the world,
they surround our steps as we journey on
towards that eternal city of light
where they sing the triumphal song.
Open our eyes to behold your glory
and free our tongues to join our song with theirs:
For great and wonderful are your deeds,
   O Lord God almighty;
just and true are your ways, O king of the ages.
To you be praise and glory, now and for ever.   **Amen.**   *12 M 1*


A shorter version of this prayer is to be found in the following
chapter as *13 M 1.*

2     Blessed are you, Sovereign God, source of light,
      giver of all things good.
      In your presence wisdom has prepared a feast;
      she calls the foolish to leave the way of darkness;
      she welcomes us with truth and goodness.
      In Jesus your light has shone out;
      his cross has brought peace to the sinful.
      Your Spirit has opened our hearts;
      with all the saints we share your light.
      Refuge of the weary, hope of the dying,
      blessed are you, Sovereign God, light in the darkness.    *12 M 2*

## Canticles

Te Deum 1–13 (ASB page 55)
or

### A SONG OF THE REDEEMED

[Response   **Salvation belongs to our God
and to the Lamb.**]

1     Behold a great multitude:
      which no one could number,

2     From every nation, from all tribes and peoples and tongues:
      standing before the throne and before the Lamb.   **[R]**

3     They were clothed in white robes
        and had palms in their hands:
      and they cried out with a loud voice,

4     'Salvation belongs to our God:
      who sits upon the throne, and to the Lamb.'   **[R]**

5     These are they who have come out of the great tribulation:
      they have washed their robes
        and made them white in the blood of the Lamb.

6    Therefore they stand before the throne of God:
     and serve him day and night within the temple.    **[R]**

7    And he who sits upon the throne:
     will shelter them with his presence.

8    They shall never again feel hunger or thirst:
     the sun shall not strike them,
          nor any scorching heat.

9    For the Lamb at the heart of the throne will be their Shepherd:
     and he will guide them to springs of living water.    **[R]**    *12 N 1*

## Patterns of Readings with Psalms and Canticles

## 1   Apostles

1    Isaiah 43.8–15
     Song of the New Creation (*The Promise* page 309)

2    Isaiah 49.1–6
     Song of the Redeemer (*The Promise* page 309)

3    Isaiah 61.1–3a
     Psalm 96

4    1 Corinthians 4.9–13
     Psalm 126

5    Ephesians 2.13–end
     Psalm 139.12–28

6    Revelation 21.1–4,9–14
     Song of God's Judgement (*The Promise* page 331)

Gospel   John 15.12–16                                    *12 P 1*

## 2  *Evangelists*

1   Deuteronomy 30.11–14
    'Listen, O heavens' (*Lent, Holy Week, Easter* page 256)

2   Isaiah 42.5–12
    Psalm 92.12–end

3   Isaiah 52.7–10
    Psalm 67

4   Isaiah 62.6–end
    Psalm 19.1–6

5   Ezekiel 1.4–14
    Song of the Faithful (*The Promise* page 320)

6   2 Corinthians 5.11—6.2
    'Great and Wonderful' (ASB page 54)

Gospel   Matthew 9.35—10.4                                    *12 P 2*

See also the pattern for Apostles and Evangelists on page 37 of *The Promise of His Glory.*


## *Ending*

> May the infinite and glorious Trinity,
> the Father, the Son, and the Holy Spirit,
> direct our life in good works,
> and after our journey through this world,
> grant us eternal rest with the saints.   **Amen.**        *12 Q 1*

# 13  THE SAINTS

Some of the material in Chapter 12, for Apostles and Evangelists, is also suitable on other saints' days.

## Invitation to Confession

1    Christ calls us to share the heavenly banquet of his love
     with all the saints in earth and heaven.
     Knowing our unworthiness and sin,
     let us ask from him both mercy and forgiveness.          *13 A 1*

2    The saints were faithful until death
     and now dwell in the heavenly kingdom for ever.
     As we celebrate their joy,
     let us bring to the Lord our sins and weaknesses,
     and ask for his mercy.                                    *13 A 2*

## Penitential Kyrie

1    Let judgement for me come forth from your presence,
     and let your eyes discern the right:
     Lord, have mercy.
     **Lord, have mercy.**

     Search my heart and visit me;
     try me by fire:
     Christ, have mercy.
     **Christ, have mercy.**

     Keep me as the apple of your eye;
     hide me under the shadow of your wing:
     Lord, have mercy.
     **Lord, have mercy.**                                     *13 B 1*

2    Lord, you are gracious and compassionate:
Lord, have mercy.
**Lord, have mercy.**

You are loving to all,
and your mercy is over all your creation:
Christ, have mercy.
**Christ, have mercy.**

Your faithful servants bless your name,
and speak of the glory of your kingdom:
Lord, have mercy.
**Lord, have mercy.**            *13 B 2*

3    You give your kingdom to the poor in spirit:
Lord, have mercy.
**Lord, have mercy.**

You satisfy those who hunger for righteousness and justice:
Christ, have mercy.
**Christ, have mercy.**

You give joy and gladness to those who mourn:
Lord, have mercy.
**Lord, have mercy.**            *13 B 3*

## Intercession

[Not every section in this intercession need be used on every occasion.]

1    In every age you have raised up holy men and women
to reflect the light of Christ and to teach us the ways of holiness.

We thank you for those who have been teachers
in the school of Christ:
give understanding to those who study
the faith the Church has handed on,
and clarity to those who communicate the gospel
in a changing world . . .

Lord, hear us.
**Lord, graciously hear us.**

We thank you for those who have been shepherds
　　of your people:
give a pastoral heart to deacons, priests and bishops,
and the needful gifts to all your people in their ministry . . .

Lord, hear us.
**Lord, graciously hear us.**

We thank you for those who have been Christian rulers
　　in the world,
and for those who carried the good news
　　to lands where it had not been before:
give wisdom to all who have power and influence
　　among the nations,
and establish God's sovereignty among people of every race . . .

Lord, hear us.
**Lord, graciously hear us.**

We thank you for those who have struggled for the poor
　　and the powerless:
give strength to all who see Christ in the oppressed
and uphold them as they work for justice and release . . .

Lord, hear us.
**Lord, graciously hear us.**

We thank you for those whom you have called to live
　　in community:
establish mutual love among those drawn into fellowship
　　in your service,
and bless with Christ's presence
　　all the communities to which our lives relate . . .

Lord, hear us.
**Lord, graciously hear us.**

We thank you for those who have lived out their vocation
    in family life:
give your grace to all who nurture children
    and all who care for the aged,
and enfold in your love all your sons and daughters . . .

Lord, hear us.
**Lord, graciously hear us.**

We thank you for those who have brought wholeness
through the medicine of the gospel:
give skill to all who minister healing and reconciliation
    in your name,
and comfort all who cry out to you from any sort of distress . . .

Lord, hear us.
**Lord, graciously hear us.**

We thank you for the noble army of martyrs
by the shedding of whose blood the Church has been enriched:
keep under your protection those who are persecuted
    for the cause of Christ,
and acknowledge, we pray,
    those who have passed through death
        trusting your promises . . .

Lord, hear us.
**Lord, graciously hear us.**

[We thank you today for . . .
As we celebrate his/her memory
    and rejoice in his/her friendship,
we ask you to bless . . .
Keep in one communion and fellowship
    all those for whom Christ died.

Lord, hear us.
**Lord, graciously hear us.]**

Hasten, Lord, the day when people will come
   from east and west,
from north and south,
and sit at table in your kingdom,
and we shall see your Son in his glory.

Merciful Father,
**accept these prayers**
**for the sake of your Son**
**our Saviour Jesus Christ.  Amen.**         *13 C 1*

[Biddings may precede this form, which should be used without
interpolation. Silence may be kept after each section.]

2     United in the company of all the faithful and looking for the
coming of the kingdom, let us offer our prayers to God, the
source of all life and holiness.

Merciful Lord, strengthen all Christian people by your Holy
Spirit, that we may live as a royal priesthood and a holy nation
to the praise of Christ Jesus our Saviour.
**Lord, have mercy.**

Bless N our bishop, and all ministers, of your Church, that by
faithful proclamation of your word we may be built on the
foundation of the apostles and prophets into a holy temple in
the Lord.
**Lord, have mercy.**

Empower us by the gift of your Holy and Life-giving Spirit that
we may be transformed into the likeness of Christ from glory
to glory.
**Lord, have mercy.**

Give to the world and its peoples the peace that comes from
above, that they may find Christ's way of freedom and life.
**Lord, have mercy.**

Hold in your embrace all who witness to your love in the
service of the poor and needy; all those who minister to the sick
and dying; and all who bring light to those in darkness.
**Lord, have mercy.**

Touch and heal all those whose lives are scarred by sin or disfigured by pain, that, raised from death to life in Christ, their sorrow may be turned to eternal joy.
**Lord, have mercy.**

Remember in your mercy those gone before us who have been well-pleasing to you from eternity; preserve us who live here in your faith, guide us to your kingdom, and grant us your peace at all times.
**Lord, have mercy.**

Hasten the day when those who fear you in every nation will come from east and west, from north and south, and sit at table in your kingdom.
**Lord, have mercy.**

And so give you thanks for N and for the whole company of your saints in glory, with whom in fellowship we join our prayers and praises; by your grace may we, like them, be made perfect in your love.
**Blessing and glory and wisdom,**
**thanksgiving and honour and power,**
**be to our God for ever and ever.   Amen.**                *13 C 2*


## Acclamation

Great is the Lord and greatly to be praised:
**there is no end of his greatness.**
One generation shall praise your works to another:
**and shall declare your power.**
All your works praise you, Lord:
**and your faithful servants bless you.**
They make known the glory of your kingdom:
**and speak of your power.**
My mouth shall speak the praise of the Lord:
**let all flesh bless his holy name for ever and ever.**        *13 D 1*

## Simple Blessing

1    God give you grace to follow his saints
in faith, and hope and love;
and the blessing . . .        *13 E 1*

2    God give you grace to follow his saints
in faith and truth and gentleness;
and the blessing . . .        *13 E 2*

3    May Christ who makes saints of sinners,
who has transformed those we remember today,
raise and strengthen you that you may transform the world;
and the blessing . . .        *13 E 3*

## Solemn Blessing

May God, who kindled the fire of his love in the hearts of the saints, pour upon you the riches of his grace. **Amen.**

May he give you joy in their fellowship and a share in their joy. **Amen.**

May he strengthen you to walk in the way of holiness and to come to the full radiance of glory. **Amen.**

And the blessing . . .        *13 F 1*

## THE EUCHARIST

## Introduction to the Peace

1    May the God of peace make you perfect and holy,
that you may be kept safe and blameless
in spirit, soul, and body,
for the coming of our Lord Jesus Christ.        *13 G 1*

2    [For Martyrs]

Now in union with Christ Jesus
you who once were far off
have been brought near
through the shedding of Christ's blood;
for he is our peace.                                    *13 G 2*


## Eucharistic Preface

1    And now we give you thanks
for the work of your grace in the life of Saint **N**
and that by the same grace you lead us in the way of holiness
setting before us the vision of your glory.
Therefore . . .                                        *13 H 1*

2    And now we give you thanks
for the hope to which you call us in your Son,
that following in the faith of all your saints,
we may run with perseverance the race that is set before us,
and with them receive the unfading crown of glory.
Therefore . . .                                        *13 H 2*

3    And now we give you thanks
because in him you have received us as your sons and daughters,
joined us in one fellowship with the saints,
and made us citizens of your kingdom.
Therefore . . .                                        *13 H 3*

4    [For Martyrs]

And now we give you thanks
that in the witness of your martyrs
who followed Christ even to death
you revealed your power made perfect in our human weakness.
Therefore . . .                                        *13 H 4*

5    [For Martyrs]

And now we give you thanks,
glorified in the assembly of your saints,
for your martyrs who bless you and praise you,
confessing before the powers of this world
the great name of your only Son.
Therefore . . .                                    *13 H 5*

## *Words at the Breaking of Bread*

1    'I am the bread of life,' says the Lord,
'whoever comes to me will never be hungry;
whoever believes in me will never thirst.'
**Taste and see that the Lord is good:**
**happy are they who trust in him.**            *13 J 1*

2    [For Martyrs]

We break this bread,
**communion in Christ's body once broken.**
Let your Church be the wheat
which bears its fruit in dying.
**If we have died with him,**
**we shall live with him;**
**if we hold firm,**
**we shall reign with him.**                *13 J 2*

## *Invitation to Communion*

I heard the voice of a great multitude crying,
Alleluia!
The Lord our God has entered into his kingdom.
**Blessed are those who are called**
   **to the supper of the Lamb.**             *13 K 1*

## Prayers after Communion

1   Father of all, you gathered us here
        around the table of your Son:
    we have shared this meal with saints
        and the whole fellowship of the household of God.
    In that new world
        where the fulness of your peace will be revealed,
    gather people of every race, language and way of life
        to share in the one eternal banquet
        of Jesus Christ our Lord.   **Amen.**                    *13 L 1*

2   Lord of heaven,
    in this eucharist you have brought us near
        to an innumerable company of angels
        and to the spirits of the saints made perfect.
    As in this food of our earthly pilgrimage
        we have shared their fellowship,
    so may we come to share their joy in heaven;
    through Jesus Christ our Lord.   **Amen.**                   *13 L 2*

3   Almighty and everlasting God,
    you have kindled the flame of love in the hearts of the saints;
    grant to us the same faith and power of love,
    that, as we rejoice in their triumphs,
    we may be sustained by their example and fellowship;
    through Christ our Lord.   **Amen.**                         *13 L 3*

4   God of mercy,
    we give thanks that on this feast of N
    you give us the bread of heaven.
    Grant us your grace in this life,
    and glory in the world which is to come.
    We ask this in the name of Jesus Christ our Lord.   **Amen.**
                                                                 *13 L 4*

5    Father,
     we thank you for your servant N,
     in whom we see the loving service of Christ.
     May we who receive these holy mysteries
     be faithful in the ministry to which you call us,
     through your Son Jesus Christ our Lord.   **Amen.**          *13 L 5*

6    [For Martyrs]

     God of courage,
     we give thanks for this holy food,
     and we praise you for your martyr N,
     who ran with perseverance
     the race that was set before him/her,
     and won the victor's wreath that does not fade;
     through Jesus Christ our Lord.   **Amen.**                  *13 L 6*


DAILY PRAYER

## *Light Prayer*

1    Blessed are you, Sovereign God of all,
     to you be glory and praise for ever!
     In the darkness of this passing age,
     your saints proclaim the glory of your kingdom,
     revealed among us in Christ, our light.
     Open our eyes to behold your presence
     and join our song with that of the saints
     in praise of all your marvellous deeds,
     Father, Son and Holy Spirit.
     **Blessed be God for ever!**                               *13 M 1*

A longer version of this prayer is found as *12 M 1.*

2    Blessed are you, Sovereign God, Saviour of all,
Goal of all prayer, source of all love.
In the place of prayer you opened Lydia's heart,
    brought her household to faith,
    and found a home for her people.
There she met the righteousness that comes from you,
    the mysterious humility of your cross,
    the love of the saints,
    and the hope of the heavenly city.
Desire of the nations, strength of the downcast,
blessed are you, Sovereign God, Light of the
    World. **Amen.**
                                 *13 M 2*

# Canticles

### 1  A FIRST SONG OF WISDOM

[Response  **The righteous sing the glories of your name.**]

1    Wisdom freed a holy people and a blameless race:
from a nation of oppressors.

2    She entered the soul of a servant of the Lord:
and withstood fearsome rulers with wonders and signs.

3    To the saints she gave the reward of her labours:
and led them by a marvellous road.  **[R]**

4    She was their shelter by day:
and a blaze of stars by night.

5    She brought them across the Red Sea:
she led them through mighty waters.

6    She swallowed their enemies in the waves:
and spat them out from the depths of the sea.  **[R]**

7    Then, Lord, the righteous sang the glories of your name:
and praised together your protecting hand;

8    For wisdom opened the mouths of the silent:
     and gave speech to the tongues of her children.   **[R]**     *13 N 1*


2  A SECOND SONG OF WISDOM

[Response **The one who meditates on wisdom
           will find gladness and a crown of rejoicing.**]

1    Blessed is the man who meditates on wisdom:
     he who reflects in his mind on her ways
         will also ponder her secrets.

2    He will be sheltered by her from the heat:
     and will dwell in the midst of her glory.   **[R]**

3    The man who fears the Lord will do this:
     and he who holds to the law will obtain wisdom.

4    She will come to meet him like a mother:
     and like the wife of his youth she will welcome him.   **[R]**

5    She will feed him with the bread of understanding:
     and give him the water of wisdom to drink.

6    He will lean on her and will not fall:
     and he will rely on her and will not be put to shame.   **[R]**

7    She will exalt him above his neighbours:
     and will open his mouth in the midst of the assembly.

8    He will find gladness and a crown of rejoicing:
     and will acquire an everlasting name.   **[R]**     *13 N 2*


3  A SONG OF PILGRIMAGE

[Response **Glory to the one who gives me wisdom!**]

1    While I was still young, before I began my travels:
     I sought for wisdom openly in my prayers.

2    I asked for her outside the temple sanctuary:
     and I shall seek her to the end.

3    She has been the delight of my heart:
      from first blossom to early fruit.  **[R]**

4    I have kept firmly to the true path:
      I have followed her steps since my youth.

5    I bowed my ear a little and received her:
      I found wisdom and was well instructed.

6    Glory to the one who gives me wisdom!
      I shall live according to her way.  **[R]**

7    From the beginning I gained understanding from her:
      therefore I shall never be deserted.

8    Because I longed to find her with all my heart:
      I have gained a good possession.

9    As my reward the Lord has given me a tongue:
      with which I shall sing his praises.  **[R]**         *13 N 3*

## 4 THE SOULS OF THE RIGHTEOUS

[Response **The souls of the righteous
are in the hands of God.**]

1    The souls of the righteous are in the hands of God:
      no torment shall ever touch them.

2    In the eyes of the unwise they seemed to have died,
        their departure was taken for defeat:
      their going from us to be a disaster;
        but they are in peace.  **[R]**

3    Though they appeared to be punished,
        their hope is rich in immortality:
      small their affliction, but great their blessing.

4    God proved and found them worthy of himself:
      like gold in a furnace he tried them,
        and accepted them as an oblation.  **[R]**

5   In the moment of God's coming
       they shall kindle into flame:
    and run like sparks among the stubble.

6   They shall govern nations and peoples:
    and the Lord shall be their ruler for ever.   **[R]**                *13 N 4*

## Patterns of Readings with Psalms and Canticles

### 1   Women Saints

1   Isaiah 61.1–3a
       Song of the Bride (*11 N 2*)

2   Proverbs 8.1–11 or
    Proverbs 31.10–end
       Psalm 119.1–8

3   Song of Solomon 4.8–12; 8.6–7
       Psalm 45.10–end

4   Ecclesiasticus 2.7–13
       Psalm 123

5   Romans 8.22–27 or
    Philippians 4.4–9
       Psalm 19.8–end

6   1 John 2.15–17 or
    2 Corinthians 10.17—11.2
       Song of the Lamb (*The Promise* page 332)

Gospel   Luke 10.38–end or
          Luke 12.32–37                                    *13 P 1*

## 2  Men Saints

1    1 Kings 19.9–18 or
Malachi 2.5–7
    Psalm 119.97–104

2    Micah 6.6–8
    Psalm 15

3    Isaiah 6.1–8
    Psalm 40.8–13

4    Ecclesiasticus 39.1–10 or
Ecclesiasticus 15.1–6
    Psalm 34.11–18

5    Wisdom 7.7–16 or
Proverbs 4.2–9
    Psalm 119.89–96

6    1 Corinthians 2.6–10,13–16 or
Philippians 3.7–14 or
2 Timothy 4.1–8
    Song of God's Grace (*The Promise* page 329)

Gospel    Matthew 25.31–40 or
    John 16.12–15            *13 P 2*

## 3  Martyrs

1    2 Esdras 2.42–end
    Psalm 126

2    Jeremiah 15.15–21
    Psalm 124

3    Ecclesiasticus 51.1–12
    Psalm 116.1–8

4    Wisdom 4.10–15 or
Jeremiah 11.18–20
    Psalm 3

5    2 Maccabees 6.18,21,24–31 or
     2 Chronicles 24.16–21
        Psalm 31.1–8,17–18

6    1 Peter 4.12–end or
     James 1.12–18 or
     Hebrews 10.32–38a
        Song of the Redeemed (*12 N 1*)

Gospel   Matthew 10.24–26 or
         Mark 8.34–38                                    *13 P 3*


# Ending

The Lord God almighty,
Father, Son, and Holy Spirit,
the holy and undivided Trinity,
guard us, save us,
and bring us to that heavenly city,
where he lives and reigns for ever and ever.   **Amen.**     *13 Q 1*

# 14 CREATION

This material is suitable for Harvest Thanksgiving and for those other times in the Christian year when there is an emphasis on creation. These include Rogationtide and Lammastide. In the ASB provision is made on the Ninth Sunday before Christmas, and, though this is lost following the calendar and lectionary in *The Promise of His Glory*, that book allows a creation festival on the last Sunday in October. Some may also want to celebrate this theme before Lent, drawing on a long association of creation with the Third Sunday before Lent, Septuagesima.

## Invitation to Confession

God's whole creation groans.
The land produces thorns and thistles and is ready for burning.
Our sin affects all around us.
We confess our sin in penitence and faith.                    14 A 1

## Penitential Kyrie

Your righteousness, Lord, is like the strong mountains,
and your justice as the great deep:
Lord, have mercy.
**Lord, have mercy.**

With you is the well of life,
and in your light shall we see light:
Christ, have mercy.
**Christ, have mercy.**

O continue your righteous dealing
   to those that are true of heart:
Lord, have mercy.
**Lord, have mercy.**                                         14 B 1

# *Intercession*

Let us pray to God, the Lord of the harvest, that he will bring
to fruition all that he desires for his creation.

Lord of the harvest,
when we lift up our eyes to perceive with Christ's eyes,
we see that the fields of the world are already white for harvest:
we pray for your Church,
that it may be spiritually equipped to reap the harvest of souls.

Lord of creation,
**in your mercy hear us.**

Lord of the harvest,
you have created the universe by your eternal Word,
and have blessed humankind in giving us dominion
    over the earth:
we pray for your world,
that we may share and conserve its resources,
and live in reverence for the creation
    and in harmony with one another.

Lord of creation,
**in your mercy hear us.**

Lord of the harvest,
whose Son has promised that the Spirit will lead us
    into all truth:
we pray for the community in which you have set us,
    for one another and for ourselves,
that we may bear the harvest of the Spirit
    in love and joy and peace.

Lord of creation,
**in your mercy hear us.**

Lord of the harvest,
though you have given the human race a rich land,
a land of streams and springs, wheat and barley,
   vines and oil and honey,
we have made by sin a world of suffering and sorrow:
we pray for those who bear the weight of affliction,
that they may come to share the life of wholeness and plenty.

Lord of creation,
**in your mercy hear us.**

Lord of the harvest,
your Christ, the first-fruits of the resurrection,
will put in the sickle for the harvest of the dead
   at the end of time:
we pray for all those who have gone before us in his peace,
that he will bring safely home all whom you have given him
and gather us all to share together
   in the banquet of the age to come.

Lord of creation,
**in your mercy hear us.**

Accept these prayers
for the sake of your Son our Saviour Jesus Christ.   **Amen.**

*14 C 1*


## Acclamation

Blessed are you, Lord God, King of the universe!
**Your word brings on the dusk of evening.**
Your wisdom creates both night and day.
**You determine the cycles of time.**
You arrange the succession of seasons
and establish the stars in their heavenly courses.
**Lord of the starry hosts is your name.**
Living and eternal God, rule over us always.
**Blessed be the Lord, whose word makes evening fall.**

*14 D 1*

# Simple Blessing

May God the Father of our Lord Jesus Christ,
who is the source of all goodness and growth,
pour his blessing upon all things created,
and upon you his children
that you may use them to his glory
   and the welfare of all peoples;
and the blessing . . .

14 E 1

## THE EUCHARIST

# Introduction to the Peace

1   Peacemakers who sow in peace
     raise a harvest of righteousness.

14 G 1

2   The harvest of the Spirit is love, joy, peace.
    If the Spirit is the source of our life,
    let the Spirit also direct its course.

14 G 2

# Eucharistic Preface

And now we give you thanks because
all things are of your making,
all times and seasons obey your laws,
but you chose to create us in your own image,
setting us over the whole world in all its wonder.
You made us stewards of your creation,
to praise you day by day
for the marvels of your wisdom and power.
Therefore . . .

14 H 1

## Words at the Breaking of Bread

Creator of all,
we have gathered many grains
and made them into this one bread.
**We look for your Church to be gathered
from the ends of the earth
into the kingdom.**

14 J 1

## Invitation to Communion

Christ is the bread which has come down from heaven.
**Lord, give us this bread for ever.**

14 K 1

## Prayers after Communion

1    Creator God,
     you give seed for us to sow,
     and bread for us to eat;
     make us thankful for what we have received,
     and do in us those generous things
     that supply your people's needs;
     so all the world may give you thanks and glory,
     in Jesus Christ our Lord.   **Amen.**

14 L 1

2    Lord of all,
     as with joy we have offered
     thanksgiving for your love in creation,
     move our hearts to be generous and wise stewards
     of the good things we enjoy;
     through Jesus Christ our Lord.   **Amen.**

14 L 2

## DAILY PRAYER

## *Light Prayer*

Blessed are you, Sovereign God, our light and our salvation,
to you be glory and praise for ever.
In the beginning you laid the foundation of the earth,
and the heavens are the work of your hands.
To dispel the darkness of our night,
you sent forth your Son, the first-born of all creation.
He is our Christ, the light of the world,
and him we acclaim, as all creation sings to you,
Father, Son and Holy Spirit.
**Blessed be God for ever.**                                    *14 M 1*

## *Canticles*

Song of Creation (ASB page 53) or

### THE CANTICLE OF THE SUN

[Response **Praised be my Lord by all his creatures.**]

1   O most high, almighty, good Lord, God:
    to you belong praise, glory, honour and all blessing.

2   Praised be my Lord by all his creatures:
    and chiefly by our brother the sun,
        who brings us the day and brings us the light.

3   Fair is he, and shines with a very great splendour:
    he points us, O Lord, to you.   **[R]**

4   Praised be my Lord by our sister the moon:
    and by the stars which you have set clear and lovely in heaven.

5   Praised be my Lord by our brother the wind:
    and by air and clouds, calms and all weather,
        by which you uphold life in all creatures.

6    Praised be my Lord by our sister water:
     who is very useful to us
          and humble and precious and clean.    [R]

7    Praised be my Lord by our brother fire,
          through whom you give light in the darkness:
     and he is bright and pleasant and very mighty and strong.

8    Praised be my Lord by our mother the earth,
          who sustains us and keeps us:
     and brings forth fruit of different kinds,
          flowers of many colours, and grass.    [R]

9    Praised be my Lord by all who pardon one another
          for your love's sake:
     and all who endure weakness and trials.

10   Blessed are they who calmly endure:
     for you, O most high, shall give them a crown.    [R]

11   Praised be my Lord by our sister the death of the body,
          from which no one escapes:
     blessed are those who are found waking by your most holy will.

12   Praise and bless the Lord, and give thanks to him:
     and serve him with great humility.    [R]                    14 N 1

# Patterns of Readings with Psalms and Canticles

## 1   Creation/Rogation

1    Deuteronomy 26.1–11
        Psalm 147.1–13

2    Job 38.1–11,16–18
        Psalm 104.25–37

3    Ezekiel 47.6–12
        Psalm 107.23–32

4    Ecclesiasticus 38.27–32
        Psalm 107.1–9

5    Acts 14.8–18
        Psalm 107.33–end

6    2 Corinthians 9.9–11a or
        1 Timothy 6.7–10,17–19
        Psalm 112

Gospel    Mark 11.22–24 or
        John 6.22–40                                        *14 P 1*


## 2    Harvest

1    Leviticus 23.26–32,39–43
        Psalm 79.8–9,11,13

2    Amos 9.13–15
        Psalm 113

3    Hosea 14.2–10
        Psalm 90.1–6,13–end

4    Nehemiah 8.1–10
        Psalm 33.1–6

5    Zechariah 8.14–19
        Psalm 141

6    Hebrews 9.2–12
        Psalm 117

Gospel    Luke 13.6–17                                    *14 P 2*


## Ending

May God who clothes the lilies and feeds the birds of the sky,
who leads the lambs to pasture and the deer to water,
who multiplied loaves and fishes and changed water into wine,
lead us, feed us, multiply us,
and change us to reflect the glory of our Creator
through all eternity.    **Amen.**                        *14 Q 1*

# 15 JUSTICE AND PEACE

## Invitation to Confession

Let us confess to God the sins and shortcomings of the world;
its pride, its selfishness, its greed;
its evil divisions and hatreds.
Let us confess our share in what is wrong,
and our failure to seek and establish that peace
which God wills for his children.                    *15 A 1*

## Penitential Kyrie

1    Lord Jesus, you wept over the sins of your city:
     Lord, have mercy.
     **Lord, have mercy.**

     Lord Jesus, you heal the wounds of sin and division,
         jealousy and bitterness:
     Christ, have mercy.
     **Christ, have mercy.**

     Lord Jesus, you bring pardon and peace to the sinner:
     Lord, have mercy.
     **Lord, have mercy.**                             *15 B 1*

2    'I was hungry and you gave me no food,
     I was thirsty and you gave me no drink.'
     Lord, have mercy.
     **Lord, have mercy.**

     'I was a stranger and you did not welcome me,
     naked and you did not clothe me.'
     Christ, have mercy.
     **Christ, have mercy.**

'I was sick and you did not visit me,
in prison, and you did not come to me.'
Lord, have mercy.
**Lord, have mercy.**

*15 B 2*

## *Intercession*

1    We bring before God our needs and the needs of his world.

Wonderful Counsellor,
give your wisdom to the rulers of the nations.

Lord, in your mercy
**hear our prayer.**

Mighty God,
make the whole world know
that the government is on your shoulders.

Lord, in your mercy
**hear our prayer.**

Everlasting Father,
establish your reign of justice and righteousness
for ever.

Lord, in your mercy
**hear our prayer.**

Prince of peace,
bring in the endless kingdom of your peace.

Lord, in your mercy
**hear our prayer.**

Almighty Lord,
**hear our prayer,**
**and fulfil your purposes in us,**
**as you accomplished your will**
**in our Lord Jesus Christ.   Amen.**

*15 C 1*

2    Almighty God,
you have promised that you will come near to us when we come
    near to you:

Cleanse our hands and purify our hearts as we bow before you
and bring before you the needs of our world, saying

Lord, in your mercy
**hear our prayer.**

We pray for one another as we meet the trials and testing of our
faith . . .
In our pain, give us perseverance.
In our ignorance, wisdom.
In our doubt, faith.

Lord, in your mercy
**hear our prayer.**

We pray for our families, neighbours and friends . . .
In our life together, give us love and humility.
Make us quick to listen and slow to anger.
Make us doers as well as hearers of your word.
Take away envy, ambition and disorder,
and make us peacemakers, full of peace and integrity.

Lord, in your mercy
**hear our prayer.**

We pray for those in need, inside and outside the Church . . .
for those who care for orphans and widows,
for those whose actions meet the needs
    of those without clothes and daily bread
    and those who wear gold rings and fine raiment.
We pray for justice in our society,
for forgiveness for our favouritism,
and for the insight to love those who are rich in faith
    yet poor in the eyes of the world.

Lord, in your mercy
**hear our prayer.**

We pray for our government and for the leaders of the
nations . . .
for those who put faith into practice and words into deeds.
Set a guard over their words
and take away the causes of quarrels and fighting.

Lord, in your mercy
**hear our prayer.**

We pray in faith for those who are sick and in trouble . . .
for time to pray,
for people to pray with,
for hands to convey your healing,
for prayer to be answered.

Lord, in your mercy
**hear our prayer.**

We rejoice in our fellowship with all those who, like Abraham,
are counted righteous before you
because faith and actions are working together . . .
Bring us together with the poor and all your saints
to inherit the kingdom you promise to those who love you.

Lord of the Church,
**hear our prayer,**
**and make us one in heart and mind**
**to serve you with joy for ever.   Amen.**          *15 C 2*

## *Acclamation*

His salvation is near to those who fear him:
his glory shall dwell in our land.
**His salvation is near to those who fear him:**
**his glory shall dwell in our land.**
I will listen to what the Lord God is saying,
for he is speaking peace to his faithful people
and to those who turn their hearts to him.
**His glory shall dwell in our land.**
Mercy and truth have met together;
righteousness and peace have kissed each other.
**His glory shall dwell in our land.**
Truth shall spring up from the earth,
and righteousness shall look down from heaven.
**His glory shall dwell in our land.**
Righteousness shall go before him,
and peace shall be a pathway to his feet.
**His salvation is near to those who fear him;**
**his glory shall dwell in our land.**                    *15 D 1*

## *Simple Blessing*

1   Now may the Lord of peace himself
        give you peace at all times and in every way.
    The Lord be with you all;
    and the blessing . . .                                *15 E 1*

2   God grant to the living, grace;
    to the departed, rest;
    to the Church, the Queen, the Commonwealth,
        and all humankind, peace and concord;
    and to us and all his servants, life everlasting;
    and the blessing . . .                                *15 E 2*

## *Solemn Blessing*

May God the Father,
who made from one every nation that occupies the earth,
bless you. **Amen.**

May God the Son,
who bought us for God from every tribe and language
    and people and nation,
bless you. **Amen.**

May God the Holy Spirit,
who brings us together in unity,
bless you. **Amen.**

And may the blessing of God almighty,
the Father, the Son and the Holy Spirit,
come down upon you and give you peace
now and always. **Amen.**                          *15 F 1*


## THE EUCHARIST

## *Introduction to the Peace*

1    God calls us to peace:
    **in God's justice is our peace.**
    Christ calls us to be God's people:
    **in Christ is our peace.**
    The peace of the Lord be . . .                 *15 G 1*

2    Blessed are those who make peace:
    they shall be called sons and daughters of God.
    We meet in the name of Christ and share his peace.   *15 G 2*

## Eucharistic Preface

1    And now we give you thanks
because you have anointed your Son as the Messiah,
the light of the nations,
and revealed him as the hope
of all who thirst for righteousness and peace.
Therefore . . .        *15 H 1*

2    And now we give you thanks,
for you are the hope of the nations,
the builder of the city that is to come.
Your love is made visible in Jesus Christ,
you bring home the lost, restore the sinner
and give dignity to the despised.
In the face of Jesus Christ
your light shines out,
flooding lives with goodness and truth,
gathering into one a divided and broken humanity.
Therefore . . .        *15 H 2*

3    And now we give you thanks
because we are your new creation in Christ:
you fill us with your Spirit,
to bring good news to the poor,
to heal the broken hearted,
to announce release to captives
and freedom to prisoners,
to proclaim the death of Christ until he comes again.
Therefore . . .        *15 H 3*

## Words at the Breaking of Bread

It is more appropriate to break the bread during the words of 'Lamb of God' than to introduce another text before or instead of that text.

## *Invitation to Communion*

Jesus is the Lamb of God
who takes away the sins of the world.
Happy are those who are called to his supper.
**Lord, I am not worthy to receive you,**
**but only say the word, and I shall be healed.**          *15 K 1*


## *Prayers after Communion*

1    Great God, you are one God,
     and you bring together what is scattered
     and mend what is broken.
     Unite us with the scattered peoples of the earth
     that we may be one family of your children.
     Bind up all our wounds,
     and heal us in spirit
     that we may be renewed as disciples
          of Jesus Christ, our Master and our Saviour.   **Amen.**   *15 L 1*

2    Lord God,
     you hold both earth and heaven in a single peace.
     Let the design of your great love
     shine on the waste of our rages and sorrows,
     and give peace to your Church,
     peace among nations,
     peace in our homes,
     and peace in our hearts,
     in Jesus Christ our Lord.   **Amen.**          *15 L 2*

3    Father in heaven,
     we pray that the joy of this celebration
     may fill our hearts
     with a new and deeper sense of your love
     for us and for your world,
     and that we may reflect your love
     by lives of service;
     through Christ our Lord.   **Amen.**          *15 L 3*

169

4    Merciful God
     we have been gathered at the table of your Son.
     Hear our prayer for all our sisters and brothers in faith
     who suffer for truth, justice, and freedom.
     Strengthen their witness
     and keep them, with us,
     under the protection of your wings.
     We ask this in the name of Jesus Christ our Lord.    **Amen.**

                                                              *15 L 4*


## DAILY PRAYER

## *Light Prayer*

     Blessed are you, Sovereign God, fountain of love,
     the suffering of your cross brings light to the nations
     and healing to all who are wounded by sin.
     In the darkness Jesus kept faith as your servant;
     he listened for your word and sustained the downcast;
     despised and rejected, he was bruised for our wrong-doing.
     Led to the slaughter like a lamb he opened not his mouth.
     He suffered like a woman in labour
     and rejoiced to see many born to new righteousness.
     His victory will be proclaimed in every generation
     and his reign of love will never come to an end.
     Blessed are you, Sovereign God,
          light in the darkness.    **Amen.**                *15 M 1*


## *Canticles*

*1* THE BEATITUDES

     [Response    **Rejoice and be glad,
                  for your reward is great in heaven.**]

1    Blessed are the poor in spirit:
     for theirs is the kingdom of heaven.

2    Blessed are those who mourn:
for they shall be comforted.   **[R]**

3    Blessed are the gentle:
for they shall inherit the earth.

4    Blessed are those who hunger and thirst for what is right:
for they shall be satisfied. **[R]**

5    Blessed are the merciful:
for mercy shall be shown to them.

6    Blessed are the pure in heart:
for they shall see God. **[R]**

7    Blessed are the peacemakers:
for they shall be called children of God.

8    Blessed are those who are persecuted
   in the cause of right:
for theirs is the kingdom of heaven. **[R]**

9    Blessed are you when others revile you and persecute you:
and utter all kinds of evil against you falsely for my sake.

10   Rejoice and be glad:
for your reward is great in heaven. **[R]**        *15 N 1*


## 2   A SONG OF PEACE

[Response **Let us walk in the light of the Lord.**]

1    Come, let us go up to the mountain of the Lord:
to the house of the God of Jacob;

2    That he may teach us his ways:
that we may walk in his paths.

3    For the law shall go out from Zion:
and the word of the Lord from Jerusalem.   **[R]**

4    He shall judge between the nations:
and settle disputes for many peoples;

5   They shall beat their swords into ploughshares:
    their spears into pruning hooks;

6   Nation shall not lift up sword against nation:
    nor ever again be trained for war.  **[R]**

*7   People of Jacob, come:
    let us walk in the light of the Lord.

* Omit this verse if the response is used.         *15 N 2*

# Patterns of Readings with Psalms and Canticles

## 1

1     Amos 5.21–24
       Psalm 85.7–end

2     Isaiah 32.1–2,12–18
       Psalm 46

3     Isaiah 58.1–9
       Psalm 72.8,9,12–14

4     1 John 4.16–end
       Psalm 145.13–end

5     1 Timothy 2.1–6
       Psalm 72.1–7

6     Colossians 3.12–15
       Song of Moses and of the Lamb (*The Promise* page 331)

Gospel   Matthew 5.38–end          *15 P 1*

## 2

1     Micah 4.1–5
       Psalm 46

2    Isaiah 10.33—11.9
       Psalm 72.1–7

3    Isaiah 42.1–7
       Psalm 85.7–end

4    1 John 3.14–18
       Psalm 145.13–end

5    James 2.5–9,12–17
       Psalm 72.8,9,12–14

6    Ephesians 2.13–18
       The Beatitudes (*15 N 1*)

Gospel   John 16.23–end          *15 P 2*

## *Ending*

May the Lord of peace give us peace
in all ways and at all times.  **Amen.**     *15 Q 1*

# 16  HEALING AND RECONCILIATION

## Invitation to Confession

1    The grace of God has dawned upon the world
       with healing for all.
    Let us come to him, in sorrow for our sins,
    seeking healing and salvation.             *16 A 1*

2    God shows his love for us in this:
    while we were still sinners Christ died for us.
    Sure of reconciliation through the death of his Son
    we confess our sins to God.             *16 A 2*

## Penitential Kyrie

1    Lord Jesus, you healed the sick:
    Lord, have mercy.
    **Lord, have mercy.**

    Lord Jesus, you forgave sinners:
    Christ, have mercy.
    **Christ, have mercy.**

    Lord Jesus, you give us yourself to heal us and bring us
       strength.
    Lord, have mercy.
    **Lord, have mercy.**             *16 B 1*

2    Lord Jesus, you came to reconcile us
    to one another and to the Father:
    Lord, have mercy.
    **Lord, have mercy.**

Lord Jesus, you heal the wounds of sin and division:
Christ, have mercy.
**Christ, have mercy.**

Lord Jesus, you intercede for us with your Father:
Lord, have mercy.
**Lord, have mercy.** *16 B 2*

## *Intercession*

1   Christ, who was born in a stable,
    give courage to all who are homeless.
    In your mercy,
    **hear our prayer.**

Christ, who fled into Egypt,
give comfort to all refugees.
In your mercy,
**hear our prayer.**

Christ, who fasted in the desert,
give relief to all who are starving.
In your mercy,
**hear our prayer.**

Christ, who hung in agony on the cross,
give strength to all who suffer.
In your mercy,
**hear our prayer.**

Christ, who died to save us,
give peace to all who seek pardon.
In your mercy,
**hear our prayer.** *16 C 1*

2   We pray for the coming of God's kingdom, saying
    Father, by your Spirit
    **bring in your kingdom.**

You came in Jesus to bring good news to the poor,
sight to the blind, freedom to captives,
and salvation to your people:
anoint us with your Spirit;
rouse us to work in his name:

Father, by your Spirit
**bring in your kingdom.**

Send us to bring help to the poor
and freedom to the oppressed:

Father, by your Spirit
**bring in your kingdom.**

Send us to tell the world
the good news of your healing love:

Father, by your Spirit
**bring in your kingdom.**

Send us to those who mourn,
to bring joy and gladness instead of grief:

Father, by your Spirit
**bring in your kingdom.**

Send us to proclaim that the time is here
for you to save your people:

Father, by your Spirit
**bring in your kingdom.**

Lord of the Church,
**hear our prayer,**
**and make us one in heart and mind**
**to serve you in Christ our Lord.    Amen.**                    *16 C 2*


## Acclamation

I saw water flowing from the threshold of the temple:
**where the river flows everything will spring to life.**

On the banks of the river grow trees bearing every kind of fruit:
**their leaves will not wither nor their fruit fail.**

Their fruit will serve for food,
their leaves for the healing of the nations:
**for the river of the water of life
flows from the throne of God and of the Lamb.**     *16 D 1*


## Simple Blessing

1    May Christ,
who out of defeat brings a new hope and a new future,
fill you with his new life;
and the blessing . . .     *16 E 1*

2    May God keep you in all your days.
May Christ shield you in all your ways.
May the Spirit bring you healing and peace.
May God the Holy Trinity drive all darkness from you
and pour upon you blessing and light.     *16 E 2*


## Solemn Blessing

The Lord bless you and keep you.  **Amen.**

The Lord make his face shine upon you,
and be gracious to you.  **Amen.**

The Lord lift up his countenance upon you
and give you peace.  **Amen.**

The Lord God almighty, Father, Son, and Holy Spirit,
the holy and undivided Trinity,
guard you, save you,
and bring you to that heavenly city,
where he lives and reigns for ever and ever.  **Amen.**     *16 F 1*

THE EUCHARIST

## Introduction to the Peace

1 Jesus says:
'Peace I leave with you. My peace I give to you.
Not as the world gives give I unto you.
Do not let your hearts be troubled, neither let them be afraid.'

*16 G 1*

2 Blessed be Christ, the prince of peace.
**He breaks down the walls that divide us:**
**praise Christ who is our peace.**
The peace of the Lord be . . .

*16 G 2*

## Eucharistic Preface

1 And now we give you thanks
because in his victory over the grave
a new age has dawned,
the long reign of sin is ended,
a broken world is being renewed,
and humanity is once again made whole.
Therefore . . .

*16 H 1*

2 And now we give you thanks
because you provide medicine to heal our sickness,
and the leaves of the tree of life
    for the healing of the nations,
anointing us with your healing power
so that we may be the first-fruits of your new creation.
Therefore . . .

*16 H 2*

# Words at the Breaking of Bread

'I am the bread of life', says the Lord.
'Whoever comes to me will never be hungry;
whoever believes in me will never thirst.'
**Taste and see that the Lord is good:**
**happy are they who trust in him.**

*16 J 1*

# Invitation to Communion

Jesus is the Lamb of God
who takes away the sins of the world.
Happy are those who are called to his supper.
**Lord, I am not worthy to receive you,**
**but only say the word, and I shall be healed.**

*16 K 1*

# Prayers after Communion

1    Eternal God,
comfort of the afflicted and healer of the broken,
you have fed us at the table of life and hope.
Teach us the ways of gentleness and peace,
that all the world may acknowledge
the kingdom of your Son Jesus Christ our Lord.    **Amen.** *16 L 1*

2    God of our salvation,
you have restored us to life,
you have brought us back again into your love,
by the triumphant death and resurrection of Christ.
Continue to heal us,
as we go to live and work
in the power of your Spirit,
to your praise and glory.    **Amen.**

*16 L 2*

3     Compassionate God,
in this eucharist you have set aside our sins
and given us your healing.
Grant that we who have been made whole
may bring your healing to this broken world,
in the name of Jesus Christ our Lord.  **Amen.**       *16 L 3*

4     Lord of all mercy,
we your faithful people have celebrated that sacrifice
   which takes away our sins and brings pardon and peace.
May our communion keep us firm
   on the foundation of the gospel
and preserve us from all sin;
through Jesus Christ our Lord.  **Amen.**       *16 L 4*

## DAILY PRAYER

## *Light Prayer*

Blessed are you, Sovereign God,
Shepherd of your pilgrim people:
their pillar of cloud by day,
their pillar of fire by night.
Stir up in us the fire of your love
which shone forth from your Son
enthroned on the cross,
that we may be cleansed of all our sins,
healed of all our infirmities,
and be made ready to come into your presence,
Father, Son and Holy Spirit.
**Blessed be God for ever.**       *16 M 1*

or the Light Prayer for Passiontide (*3 M 1*)

# Canticle

## A SONG OF THE WILDERNESS

[Response **The ransomed of the Lord
shall return with singing.**]

1    The wilderness and the dry land shall rejoice:
     the desert shall burst into song.

2    They shall see the glory of the Lord:
     the splendour of our God. **[R]**

3    Strengthen the weary hands:
     make firm the feeble knees.

4    Say to the anxious, be strong, fear not:
     your God is coming in judgement to save you. **[R]**

5    Then shall the eyes of the blind be opened:
     and the ears of the deaf unstopped;

6    Then the lame shall leap like the deer:
     and the tongue of the dumb sing for joy. **[R]**

7    For waters shall spring up in the wilderness:
     and streams flow in the desert.

8    The ransomed of the Lord shall return with singing:
     crowned with everlasting joy.

9    They shall obtain joy and gladness:
     and sorrow and sighing shall flee away.                *16 N 1*

# Patterns of Readings with Psalms and Canticles

## 1

1    Genesis 45.1–5,12–15
         Psalm 105.1–5,16–22

2    1 Samuel 24.(1–8)9–17
         Psalm 71.1–8

3    Isaiah 55.6–9
      Psalm 51.1–9

4    Ezekiel 18.21–23,30–end
      Psalm 103.1–4,11–18

5    1 John 1.5—2.2
      Psalm 130

6    1 Corinthians 13
      Song of God's Grace (*The Promise* page 329)

Gospel    Matthew 18.21–end or
          Luke 7.36–end          *16 P 1*

## 2

1    Genesis 31.24–30; 33.1–4
      Psalm 105.1–11

2    2 Samuel 9
      Psalm 73.23–end

3    Joel 2.12–18
      Psalm 51.10–17

4    Jonah 3
      Psalm 130

5    Galatians 6.1–5
      Psalm 85.7–end

6    Colossians 3.12–15
      Song of Redemption (*The Promise* page 328)

Gospel    Matthew 5.43–end
          Luke 15.11–end         *16 P 2*

## Ending

The Lord God almighty is our Father:
**he loves us and cares tenderly for us.**
The Lord Jesus Christ is our Saviour:
**he has redeemed us and will defend us to the end.**
The Lord, the Holy Spirit, is among us:
**he will lead us in God's holy way.**
**To God almighty, Father, Son and Holy Spirit,**
**be praise and glory today and for ever.   Amen.**        *16 Q 1*

# 17  BAPTISM

This material is suitable both for an occasion when baptism is the particular focus in a service, and also on ordinary Sundays when Baptism is celebrated during the liturgy. However care should be taken not to detract from the cycle of the Christian year by substituting too much of this material for seasonal provision, especially at key times and seasons in the cycle.

Some of this material is also suitable for use at Confirmation.

## Invitation to Confession

> Because God was merciful,
> he saved us through the water of rebirth,
> and the renewing power of the Holy Spirit.
> But through sin we have fallen away from our baptism.
> Let us return to the Lord and renew our faith in his promises
> by confessing our sins in penitence.                    *17 A 1*

## Penitential Kyrie

> Wash me thoroughly from my wickedness
>     and cleanse me from my sin:
> Lord, have mercy.
> **Lord, have mercy.**
>
> Create in me a clean heart, O God,
>     and renew a right spirit within me:
> Christ, have mercy.
> **Christ, have mercy.**
>
> Cast me not away from your presence,
>     and take not your Holy Spirit from me:
> Lord, have mercy.
> **Lord, have mercy.**                                   *17 B 1*

## *Intercession*

The bracketed section in this Intercession is particularly appropriate if there are no Prayers of Penitence. This Intercession could be used in procession to or from the font. The final collect is probably best omitted where the Intercession leads into the Baptism, but appropriate when it follows the Baptism and leads into the Greeting of Peace.

God the Father,
**have mercy on us.**

God the Son,
**have mercy on us.**

God the Holy Spirit,
**have mercy on us.**

Holy, blessed, and glorious Trinity,
**have mercy on us.**

By the mystery of your holy incarnation;
by your birth, childhood, and obedience;
by your baptism in the River Jordan,
**good Lord, deliver us.**

By your agony and trial;
by your cross and passion;
and by your precious death and burial,
**good Lord, deliver us.**

By your mighty resurrection;
by your glorious ascension;
and by your sending of the Holy Spirit,
**good Lord, deliver us.**

Govern and direct your holy Church; fill it with love and truth;
and grant it that unity which is your will.
**Lord, have mercy.**

Give us boldness to make disciples of all the nations,
baptizing them in the name of the Father,
and of the Son, and of the Holy Spirit.
**Lord, have mercy.**

Keep in safety those (to be) baptized today,
that all things belonging to the Spirit may live and grow in
  them.
**Lord, have mercy.**

Guide the leaders of the nations into the ways of peace and
  justice.
**Lord, have mercy.**

Help and comfort the lonely, the bereaved, and the oppressed.
**Lord, have mercy.**

Heal the sick in body and mind,
and provide for the homeless, the hungry, and the destitute.
**Lord, have mercy.**

Hear us as we remember those who have died in the peace of
  Christ,
and grant us with them a share in your eternal kingdom.
**Lord, have mercy.**

[Give us true repentance;
forgive us our sins of negligence and ignorance
and our deliberate sin
and grant us the grace of your Holy Spirit
to amend our lives according to your holy word.

**Holy God,**
**holy and strong,**
**holy and immortal,**
**have mercy upon us.]**

God,
through your only Son
you have hallowed the waters of baptism
to bring us to a new birth
and anointed him with your Spirit
in the descent of the dove.
Keep your Church always safe from evil,
direct our lives
and open the door of your kingdom
to all who are waiting to enter;
through Jesus Christ our Lord.  **Amen.**                    *17 C 1*

2    God and Father of us all,
in Christ you give us one Lord, one faith, one baptism:
look in your love upon the Church,
    the fellowship of the baptized,
and renew her life in unity and peace . . .

In faith we pray.
**We pray to you our God.**

Your Christ has commanded us to go and teach all nations,
baptizing them in the name of the Father,
    the Son and the Holy Spirit:
look in your love upon the world, redeemed by his blood,
and work out your purpose for the whole creation . . .

In faith we pray.
**We pray to you our God.**

As a mother brings her child to birth in pain and yet in joy,
you bring us to new birth in the waters of baptism
and make us your own by adoption and grace:
look in your love upon each one of your children,
and bless with your presence every home and every family . . .

In faith we pray.
**We pray to you our God.**

We have accepted the baptism with which Christ was baptized,
your children suffer various trials, testing their faith,
as they await the salvation of their souls:
look in your love upon those who walk in deep darkness
and those who suffer beyond endurance . . .

In faith we pray.
**We pray to you our God.**

Christ is risen, the first-fruits of the harvest of the dead.
In baptism we die with him
   in order that we may be alive with him:
look in your love on all who are passing
   through the deep waters of death . . .
May they walk in newness of life.

In faith we pray.
**We pray to you our God.**

Grant, Lord,
that we who are baptized into the death
of your Son our Saviour Jesus Christ
may continually put to death our evil desires
and be buried with him;
that through the grave and gate of death
we may pass to our joyful resurrection;
through his merits, who died and was buried
   and rose again for us,
your Son Jesus Christ our Lord.   **Amen.**       *17 C 2*


## Acclamation

1    Since we have died with Christ,
     **we believe that we shall also live with him.**
     For we know that Christ has been raised from the dead
     **and will never die again.**
     We were baptized into union with his death;
     **and have set out on a new life with the risen Christ.**   *17 D 1*

2    The Father's voice bears witness to the Son.
     **God the Holy Trinity has revealed himself to us.**
     The Son bows his head beneath the Baptist's stream.
     **God the Holy Trinity has revealed himself to us.**
     The Spirit as a dove descends from the heavens.
     **God the Holy Trinity has revealed himself to us.**
     Submitting to John's baptism, Christ delivers us from bondage.
     **God the Holy Trinity has revealed himself to us.**    *17 D 2*


## Simple Blessing

1    The God of all grace,
     who called you to his eternal glory in Christ Jesus,
     establish, strengthen and settle you in the faith;
     and the blessing . . .                                  *17 E 1*

2    May God, who in Christ gives us a spring of water
     welling up to eternal life,
     perfect in you the image of his glory;
     and the blessing . . .                                  *17 E 2*


## Solemn Blessing

     May the Lord of his great mercy bless you,
     and give you understanding of his wisdom and grace.   **Amen.**

     May he nourish you with the riches of the catholic faith,
     and make you persevere in all good works.   **Amen.**

     May he keep your steps from wandering,
     and direct you into the paths of love and peace.   **Amen.**

     And the blessing . . .                                  *17 F 1*

## THE EUCHARIST

# Introduction to the Peace

1   We are the Body of Christ.
    In the one Spirit we were all baptized into one body.
    Let us then pursue all that makes for peace
    and builds up our common life.                    *17 G 1*

2   God has made us one in Christ.
    He has set his seal upon us,
    and as a pledge of what is to come
    has given the Spirit to dwell in our hearts.      *17 G 2*

# Eucharistic Preface

1   And now we give you thanks
    because through baptism we have been buried with Christ
    so that we may rise with him to the new life.
    Therefore . . .                                   *17 H 1*

2   And now we give you thanks
    because by water and the Holy Spirit
    you have made us in him a new people
    to show forth your glory.
    Therefore . . .                                   *17 H 2*

3   And now we give you thanks
    because you celebrated your new gift of baptism
    by signs and wonders at the Jordan.
    Your voice was heard from heaven
    to awaken faith in the presence among us
        of your Word made flesh.
    Your Spirit was seen as a dove,
    revealing Jesus as your servant,
    and anointing him with joy as the Christ,
    sent to bring to the poor the good news of salvation.

Therefore, as we celebrate the union of earth and heaven,
we rejoice to echo songs of the angels in heaven
for ever praising and saying:
**Holy, holy, holy Lord . . .**                    *17 H 3*

4    And now we give you thanks
because by water and the Holy Spirit
you have made us a holy people
in Jesus Christ our Lord;
you renew that mystery in bread and wine
to show forth your glory in all the world.
Therefore . . .                              *17 H 4*

## Words at the Breaking of Bread

Lord, we died with you on the cross.
**Now we are raised to new life.**
We were buried in your tomb.
**Now we share in your resurrection.**
Live in us, that we may live in you.            *17 J 1*

## Invitation to Communion

Draw near with faith.
Receive the body of our Lord Jesus Christ
    which he gave for you,
and his blood which he shed for you.
Eat and drink in remembrance that he died for you,
and feed on him in your hearts by faith with thanksgiving. *17 K 1*

## *Prayers after Communion*

1    God of our pilgrimage,
you have led us to the living water.
Refresh and sustain us
as we go forward on our journey,
in the name of Jesus Christ our Lord.  **Amen.**        *17 L 1*

2    Father, in baptism we die to sin,
rise again to new life,
and find our true place in your living body.
Send us out sealed in Christ's blood
   of the new covenant,
to bring healing and reconciliation
   to this wounded world,
through Jesus Christ our Lord.  **Amen.**        *17 L 2*

3    Lord God,
by our baptism into the death and resurrection
   of your Son Jesus Christ
we have been born again to be your children
and heirs of eternal life;
strengthen us by your Spirit
   to live in newness of life all our days;
through the same Christ our Lord.  **Amen.**        *17 L 3*

4    O God our Saviour,
as in baptism we are united with Christ,
so may this memorial of our redemption
help us to persevere in faith and love;
through Jesus Christ our Lord.  **Amen.**        *17 L 4*

DAILY PRAYER

## *Light Prayer*

Blessed are you, Sovereign God, joyful Trinity,
one God in the dance of holy light,
three persons in the perfect unity of love,
unchanging in being, active in mercy.
Foreshadowed in the anointing of David,
your mystery was made manifest in the baptism of Jesus.
The Son took his stand with sinners;
the Spirit led him to the service of the cross.
The reign of peace dawns in our darkness;
the fellowship of love is opened for all.
Light of the city that is to come,
fountain of beauty, source of all joy,
blessed are you, eternal God,
   Holy and undivided Trinity.  **Amen.**

*17 M 1*

## *Canticles*

### *1* A SONG OF SALVATION

[Response  **I will trust and will not be afraid.**]

1    Behold God is my salvation:
     I will trust and not be afraid.

2    For the Lord God is my strength and my song:
     and he has become my salvation. **[R]**

3    With joy you will draw water:
     from the wells of salvation.

4    On that day you will say:
     'Give thanks to the Lord, call upon his name.

5    Make known his deeds among the nations:
     proclaim that his name is exalted. **[R]**

6   Sing praises to the Lord, for he has triumphed gloriously:
    let this be known in all the earth.

7   Shout and sing for joy, you that dwell in Zion:
    for great in your midst is the Holy One of Israel.'   **[R]**     *17 N 1*


*2*   A SONG OF THE HEAVENLY CITY

[Response   **The servants of God shall see his face.**]

1   I saw no temple in the city:
    for its temple is the Lord God and the Lamb.

2   And the city has no need of sun or moon to shine upon it:
    for the glory of God illuminates it,
        and the Lamb is its true light. **[R]**

3   The nations shall walk by its light:
    and the rulers of the earth shall bring their glory into it.

4   Its gates will never be shut by day,
        nor shall there be any night:
    God's people shall bring into it
        the glory and honour of the nations. **[R]**

5   Then the angel showed me the river of the water of life:
    flowing as bright as crystal
        from the throne of God and of the Lamb.

6   And by the side of the river stood the tree of life:
    and the leaves of the tree are for the healing of the nations.

7   The throne of God and of the Lamb shall be there:
    the servants of God shall offer worship,
        and they shall see God's face. **[R]**                     *17 N 2*


# Pattern of Readings with Psalms and Canticles

1   Genesis 17.1–8
    Psalm 27.1–8,16,17

2     Deuteronomy 30.15–end
      Psalm 34.1–3,8,11–18

3     Joshua 24.1–2,15–25
      Psalm 32.1–8,12

4     Jeremiah 31.31–34
      Psalm 89.1–4,21–27

5     Acts 8.26–38
      Psalm 100

6     1 Peter 4.4–5,9–10
      Song of God's Grace (*The Promise* page 329)

Gospel    Matthew 28.18–end                 *17 P 1*

## *Ending*

The Holy Trinity,
in whose name we were baptized,
preserve us,
members of Christ,
children of God,
inheritors of the kingdom of heaven,
saved by the waters,
and filled with the Spirit.
**Glory to God,**
**Father, Son and Holy Spirit.**             *17 Q 1*

# 18 THE WORD

This material may be used at any Service of the Word or any occasion when the word of God in Scripture is the particular focus of worship. Traditionally the Second Sunday in Advent has had this emphasis. *The Promise of His Glory* advocates instead a date in October. There are many occasions when this material would be suitable.

## Invitation to Confession

The word of God is living and active.
It judges the thoughts and intentions of the heart.
All is open and laid bare before the eyes of him
    to whom we give account.
We confess our sins in penitence and faith.

*18 A 1*

## Penitential Kyrie

1    May your loving kindness come to me, O Lord,
     and your salvation according to your word:
     Lord, have mercy.
     **Lord, have mercy.**

     Your word is a lantern to my feet and a light to my path:
     Christ, have mercy.
     **Christ, have mercy.**

     O let your mercy come to me that I may live,
     for your law is my delight:
     Lord, have mercy.
     **Lord, have mercy.**

*18 B 1*

2    We have not held out the word of life
     in a dark and twisted world:
     Lord, have mercy.
     **Lord, have mercy.**

We have failed to share our bread with the hungry:
Christ, have mercy.
**Christ, have mercy.**

We have closed our hearts to the love of God:
Lord, have mercy.
**Lord, have mercy.**                                              *18 B 2*

## *Intercession*

Gracious God, fountain of all wisdom,
we pray for all Christian people;
for Bishop N,
and for those who teach and guard the faith . . .
May the word of Christ dwell richly in our hearts,
and knit us together in the bond of your love.

Hear us.
**Hear us, good Lord.**

We pray for the leaders of the nations,
and for those in authority under them . . .
Give them the gift of your wisdom,
and a right discernment in all things.

Hear us.
**Hear us, good Lord.**

We pray for . . . (city/town/village/community);
for those who live and work here,
and for those who visit this place . . .
Speak your word of peace in our midst,
and help us to serve one another as Christ has served us.

Hear us.
**Hear us, good Lord.**

We pray for those who do not believe,
and yet who long to know you, the very Word of life . . .
Open their ears to hear your voice,
and open their hearts to the knowledge of your love in Christ.

Hear us.
**Hear us, good Lord.**

We pray for those bowed down with grief, fear or sickness . . .
May your living Word bring comfort and healing
to all those in need.

Hear us.
**Hear us, good Lord.**

We give thanks for all those who have died
in the faith of Christ . . .
and we rejoice with (N and) all your saints,
trusting in the promise of your word fulfilled.

Lord of the Church,
**hear our prayer,**
**and make us one in heart and mind**
**to serve you with joy for ever.   Amen.**                    *18 C 1*


## Acclamation

Come to me and listen to my words:
hear me, and you shall have life.
**Come to me and listen to my words:**
**hear me, and you shall have life.**
The law of the Lord is perfect, reviving the soul:
the command of the Lord is true and makes wise the simple.
**Hear me, and you shall have life.**
The precepts of the Lord are right and rejoice the heart:
the commandment of the Lord is pure
and gives light to the eyes.
**Hear me, and you shall have life.**

The fear of the Lord is clean and endures for ever:
the judgements of the Lord are unchanging
  and righteous every one.
**Hear me, and you shall have life.**
More to be desired are they than gold, even much fine gold:
sweeter also than honey that drips from the comb.
**Come to me and listen to my words:**
**hear me, and you shall have life.**                    *18 D 1*


## Simple Blessing

Go now in peace,
knowing that you have been born again,
not of perishable seed, but of imperishable,
through the living and enduring word of God;
and the blessing . . .                                   *18 E 1*


THE EUCHARIST

## Introduction to the Peace

God will speak peace to his people,
to those who turn to him in their hearts.               *18 G 1*


## Eucharistic Preface

1    And now we give you thanks
     because the wisdom of your word sustains all things,
     and reveals you to us in your fulness.
     Therefore . . .                                     *18 H 1*

2    And now we give you thanks
because in the incarnation of the Word
a new light has dawned upon the world;
you have become one with us
that we might become one with you
   in your glorious kingdom.
Therefore . . .            *18 H 2*

## Words at the Breaking of Bread

How sweet are your words to my tongue;
**sweeter than honey to my mouth.**
I am the bread of life, says the Lord.
**Taste and see that the Lord is good.**    *18 J 1*

## Invitation to Communion

Jesus is the Lamb of God who takes away the sins of the world.
Happy are those who are called to his supper.
**Lord, I am not worthy to receive you,**
**but only say the word, and I shall be healed.**    *18 K 1*

## Prayers after Communion

1    Almighty God,
by whose command time runs its course;
forgive our impatience,
perfect our faith,
and, while we wait for the fulfilment of your promises,
grant us to have a good hope because of your word;
through Jesus Christ our Lord.  **Amen.**    *18 L 1*

2    God of glory,
     you nourish us with your word
     which is the bread of life.
     Fill us with your Holy Spirit,
     that through us the light of your glory
     may shine in all the world.
     We ask this in the name of Jesus Christ.    **Amen.**        *18 L 2*

3    Lord God,
     you feed us with the living bread from heaven;
     you renew our faith,
     increase our hope,
     and strengthen our love.
     Teach us to hunger
     for Christ who is the true and living bread,
     and to live by every word
     that comes from your mouth,
     through Jesus Christ our Lord.    **Amen.**        *18 L 3*


DAILY PRAYER

## *Light Prayer*

     Blessed are you, O Lord our God, ruler of the universe!
     You led your people Israel by a pillar of cloud by day
     and a pillar of fire by night.
     Enlighten our darkness by the light of your Christ.
     May his word be a lamp to our feet and a light to our path;
     for you are full of loving kindness for your whole creation,
     and we, your creatures, glorify you,
     Father, Son, and Holy Spirit,
     now and for ever.    **Amen.**        *18 M 1*

## Canticle

### A SONG OF THE WORD

[Response **Seek the Lord while he may be found.**]

1    Seek the Lord while he may be found:
call on him while he is near.

2    Let the wicked abandon their ways:
and the unrighteous their thoughts.

3    Turn back to the Lord, who will have mercy:
to our God, who will richly pardon. [**R**]

4    'For my thoughts are not your thoughts:
neither are your ways my ways', says the Lord.

5    'As the heavens are higher than the earth:
so are my ways higher than your ways
    and my thoughts than your thoughts. [**R**]

6    As the rain and snow come down from heaven:
and return not again but water the earth,

7    bringing forth life and giving growth:
seed for sowing and bread to eat,

8    so is my word that goes out from my mouth:
it does not return to me empty,

9    But it will accomplish my purpose:
and succeed in the task I give it.' [**R**]        *18 N 1*

## Patterns of Readings with Psalms and Canticles

## 1

1    Deuteronomy 6.20–25
      Psalm 119.81–88

2    1 Samuel 28.3–20
        Psalm 119.89–96

3    Isaiah 30.8–21
        Psalm 119.105–112

4    Isaiah 55.1–11
        Psalm 119.121–128

5    Proverbs 3.1–8
        Psalm 119.129–136

6    1 Timothy 3.14—4.8
        Psalm 119.169–end

Gospel    Luke 4.14–21                                    *18 P 1*


# 2

1    Deuteronomy 5.1–21
        Psalm 119.1–8

2    1 Kings 22.1–17
        Psalm 119.9–16

3    Amos 8.4–12
        Psalm 119.17–24

4    Jeremiah 36.9–26
        Psalm 119.33–40

5    Isaiah 64.1–7
        Psalm 119.49–56

6    Romans 15.4–13
        Psalm 119.65–72

Gospel    John 5.36b–end                                  *18 P 2*

## *Ending*

Hear the teaching of Jesus:
'Blessed are those who hear the word of God and obey it.'
Go now to do God's will.
The Lord bless you.   **Amen.**                    *18 Q 1*

# 19 EUCHARIST

This material is not intended for use at every eucharist, but for when the celebration is designed to reflect particularly upon the sacrament itself. One use would be with the 'propers' that the ASB gives for the Day of Thanksgiving for the Institution of Holy Communion. This is the Thursday after Trinity Sunday, and the day often called 'Corpus Christi'.

## Invitation to Confession

[You who truly and earnestly repent you of your sins,
and are in love and charity with your neighbours,
and intend to lead a new life,
following the commandments of God,
and walking from henceforth in his holy ways;]
draw near with faith,
and take this holy sacrament to your comfort;
and make your humble confession to almighty God.  *19 A 1*

## Penitential Kyrie

1   Like as the hart longs for flowing streams,
so longs my soul for you, O God:
Lord, have mercy.
**Lord, have mercy.**

O send out your light and your truth,
that they may lead me:
Christ, have mercy.
**Christ, have mercy.**

May we come to your altar, O God,
the God of our salvation:
Lord, have mercy.
**Lord, have mercy.**  *19 B 1*

2    Lord Jesus, you raise us to new life:
     Lord, have mercy.
     **Lord, have mercy.**

     Lord Jesus, you forgive our sins:
     Christ, have mercy.
     **Christ, have mercy.**

     Lord Jesus, you feed us with your body and blood:
     Lord, have mercy.
     **Lord, have mercy.**                              *19 B 2*


## Intercession

     We pray to the Lord, saying:
     In faith we pray:
     **we pray to you our God.**

     Lord, listen to the prayers of your people gathered at your table.

     In faith we pray:
     **we pray to you our God.**

     Here, where we celebrate how Christ gave us his body
         to be our spiritual food:
     Listen as we pray for his body the Church
         spread throughout the world . . .

     In faith we pray:
     **we pray to you our God.**

     Here, where we recognize the presence of Christ
         who takes away the sin of the world:
     Listen as we pray for that world
     and for its peoples for whom his blood was shed . . .

     In faith we pray:
     **we pray to you our God.**

Here, where we come together as Christ gathered
  with his friends
  to give us this meal of holy fellowship:
Listen as we pray for all whom you have given us,
  our friends and all whose lives are joined with ours . . .

In faith we pray:
**we pray to you our God.**

Here, where we remember the night of Christ's agony and trial:
Listen as we pray for all who share his sufferings
  through fear or pain or distress of many kinds . . .

In faith we pray:
**we pray to you our God.**

Here, where we join our praises
  with the whole company of heaven:
Listen as we pray for all who have trusted Christ's promise
  to raise up on the last day
    those who eat his flesh and drink his blood . . .

In faith we pray:
**we pray to you our God.**

Lord, fill our hunger with the good food that lasts,
the bread of God which comes down from heaven
and gives life to the world,
Jesus Christ your Son our Lord.  **Amen.**      *19 C 1*

## Acclamation

I am the bread of life,
anyone who comes to me shall not hunger,
anyone who believes in me shall never thirst.
**Alleluia! Lord, give us this bread always.**
The bread of God comes down from heaven,
and gives life to the world.
**Alleluia! Lord, give us this bread always.**
Anyone who eats my flesh and drinks my blood
has eternal life
and I will raise them up on the last day.
**Alleluia! Lord, give us this bread always.**
It is the Spirit that gives life; the flesh is of no avail.
The words I speak, they are spirit and they are life.
**Alleluia! Lord, give us this bread always.**        *19 D 1*

## Simple Blessing

Christ, who has nourished us with himself the living bread,
make you one in praise and love,
and raise you up at the last day;
and the blessing . . .        *19 E 1*

## Solemn Blessing

May the Father,
who fed his children with bread and honey in the wilderness,
strengthen you in your pilgrimage to the Promised Land.
**Amen.**

May the Son,
who gave his flesh for food and his blood for drink,
keep you in eternal life and raise you up on the last day.
**Amen.**

May the Holy Spirit,
who leads us into all truth,
help you discern the Lord's body
and empower you to proclaim his death until he comes.
**Amen.**
And the blessing . . . 19 F 1

## THE EUCHARIST

## *Introduction to the Peace*

1 We are the body of Christ.
By one Spirit we were all baptized into one body.
Endeavour to keep the unity of the Spirit
in the bond of peace. 19 G 1

2 Our Lord Jesus Christ says,
If, when you are bringing your gift to the altar,
you remember your brother or sister
has a grievance against you,
leave your gift where it lies before the altar.
Go, make peace;
and only then come and offer your gift. 19 G 2

## *Eucharistic Preface*

1 And now we give you thanks
because when his hour had come,
in his great love he gave this supper to his disciples,
that we might proclaim his death,
and feast with him in his kingdom.
Therefore . . . 19 H 1

2    And now we give you thanks,
because having loved his own that were in the world
he loved them unto the end;
and on the night before he suffered,
sitting at meat with his disciples,
instituted these holy mysteries;
that we, redeemed by his death
   and restored to life by his resurrection,
might be partakers of his divine nature.
Therefore . . .               *19 H 2*

3    And now we give you thanks
because by water and the Holy Spirit
you have made us a holy people
in Jesus Christ our Lord;
you renew that mystery in bread and wine
to show forth your glory in all the world.
Therefore . . .               *19 H 3*

4    And now we give you thanks
because at the last supper
as he sat at table with his apostles
he gave us this memorial of his passion
to bring us its saving power until the end of time.
In this sacrament you feed your people
and strengthen them in holiness,
so that the family of humankind
may come to walk in the light of one faith,
in one communion of love.
Therefore . . .               *19 H 4*

## *Words at the Breaking of Bread*

Creator of all,
we have gathered many grains
and made them into this one bread.
**We look for your Church to be gathered
from the ends of the earth
into the kingdom.**         *19 J 1*

## Invitation to Communion

Christ is the bread which has come down from heaven.
**Lord, give us this bread for ever.**                    19 K 1

## Prayers after Communion

1    God of truth,
     we have seen with our eyes
     and touched with our hands
     the bread of life.
     Strengthen our faith
     that we may grow in love for you
     and for each other;
     through Jesus Christ our risen Lord.  **Amen.**        19 L 1

2    Lord,
     by your mercy we have feasted upon the bread of life,
     and have shared the cup of salvation.
     Help us so to live out our days
     that our lives may proclaim your wonders;
     through Jesus Christ our Lord.  **Amen.**               19 L 2

3    Lord,
     you feed your children with the true manna,
     the living bread from heaven;
     let his holy food support us through our earthly pilgrimage
     until we come to the place
        where there is neither hunger nor thirst;
     through Christ our Lord.  **Amen.**                     19 L 3

4    Praise to you, our God and Father,
     you have fed us with the bread of heaven
     and quenched our thirst from the true vine.
     Hear our prayer, that being grafted into Christ,
     we may grow together in unity
     and feast with him in his kingdom;
     through Jesus Christ our Lord.  **Amen.**               19 L 4

DAILY PRAYER

## *Light Prayer*

The Light Prayer for Pentecost (*6 M 1*) is suitable.

## *Canticle*

### A SONG OF THE BREAD OF HEAVEN

[Response **Jesus Christ is the bread of heaven.**]

1   You gave your people the food of angels:
    and sent them bread from heaven.

2   It was ready to eat, though they did no work:
    it was rich in delights, suiting every taste.   **[R]**

3   The food which you gave:
    showed your sweetness towards your children.

4   It satisfied the desire of those who ate:
    and was flavoured as each one wished,   **[R]**

5   that the children you love might learn
        that they are not fed by various crops:
    it is your word which sustains all who trust in you.   **[R]**   *19 N 1*

## *Patterns of Readings with Psalms and Canticles*

### *1*

1   Exodus 16.2–15
    Psalm 78.1–8,21–24

2   Deuteronomy 8.1–3,14–16
    Psalm 23

3   1 Kings 19.1–8
    Psalm 34.3–10

4    2 Kings 4.42–44
      Psalm 145.10–18

5    Revelation 19.1–2a,4–9
      Psalm 111

6    1 Corinthians 10.1–17 or 16–17
      The Song of Christ's Glory (ASB page 67)

Gospel   John 6.22–35                                              19 P 1


## 2

1    Genesis 14.18–20
      Psalm 110

2    Exodus 24.3–8
      Psalm 147.12–end

3    Proverbs 9.1–6
      Psalm 34.3–10

4    Acts 2.42–end
      Psalm 42

5    Revelation 3.14–end
      Psalm 43

6    Hebrews 9.11–15
      A Song of God's Grace (*The Promise* page 329)

Gospel   Mark 14.12–25                                            19 P 2


## Ending

> Wisdom has set her table;
> she calls from the highest place in the city,
> 'Come, eat my bread and drink the wine I have mixed.
> Leave your foolishness; walk in the way of understanding.'
> **I will go to the altar of God,**
> **even to the God of my joy and gladness.**                    19 Q 2

# 20 MINISTRY

This material is suitable at ordinations, at other occasions when ministers, ordained or lay, are blessed and commissioned, on Ember Days, and when a congregation is reflecting on the meaning of Christian ministry.

## Invitation to Confession

'I set no store by life:
I only want to finish the race and complete the task
which the Lord has assigned to me,
of bearing witness to the gospel of God's grace.'
Let us confess our failure to live up to our calling.            *20 A 1*

## Penitential Kyrie

1    Lord Jesus, you are the Good Shepherd.
     You rescue us and save us:
     Lord, have mercy.
     **Lord, have mercy.**

     Lord Jesus, we follow your voice and not a stranger's.
     You lead us in and out to pasture:
     Christ, have mercy.
     **Christ, have mercy.**

     Lord Jesus, when we are attacked you do not abandon us.
     You lay down your life for your sheep:
     Lord, have mercy.
     **Lord, have mercy.**                                        *20 B 1*

2    Sovereign Lord, you made the heaven and the earth
     and the sea and everything in them:
     in our dealing with your creation,
     Lord, have mercy.
     **Lord, have mercy.**

     You anointed your holy Servant Jesus.
     Nations and peoples raged against him and plotted his death:
     in our following of your Son,
     Christ, have mercy.
     **Christ, have mercy.**

     You spoke by the Holy Spirit
     through the mouths of your servants:
     in our hearing of your word,
     Lord, have mercy.
     **Lord, have mercy.**                                    *20 B 2*

## Intercession

     We pray for the use of God's gifts to his Church, saying
     Jesus, Lord of your Church,
     **in your mercy hear us.**

     God our Father,
     you give us gifts that we may work together
     in the service of your Son:

     Bless those who lead,
     that they may be firm in faith,
     yet humble before you:

     Jesus, Lord of your Church,
     **in your mercy hear us.**

     Bless those who teach,
     that they may increase our understanding,
     and be open to your word for them:

     Jesus, Lord of your Church,
     **in your mercy hear us.**

Bless those who minister healing,
that they may bring wholeness to others,
yet know your healing in themselves:

Jesus, Lord of your Church,
**in your mercy hear us.**

Bless those through whom you speak,
that they may proclaim your word in power,
yet open their ears to your gentle whisper:

Jesus, Lord of your Church,
**in your mercy hear us.**

Bless those who work in your world today
that in the complexity of their daily lives
they may live for you, fulfil your purposes,
and seek your kingdom first.

Jesus, Lord of your Church,
**in your mercy hear us.**

Bless those who feel they have no gifts or value
and those who are powerless in this world's eyes,
that they may share their experience
    of the work of your Spirit.

Lord of the Church,
**hear our prayer,**
**and make us one in heart and mind**
**to serve you with joy for ever.   Amen.**                    *20 C 1*


## Acclamation

There are varieties of gifts:
**but the same Spirit.**
There are varieties of service:
**but the same Lord.**
There are different kinds of working:
**but the same God is at work in all.**

There is one body, one Spirit, one hope in God's call:
**one Lord, one faith, one baptism.**
There is one God, Father of all, over all and in all:
**to whom Christ ascended on high.**
And through his Spirit he gives us gifts:
**some are apostles, some are his prophets;**
evangelists, pastors and teachers he gives us:
**so that we can minister together**
to build up his body:
**to be mature in the fulness of Christ.**                    *20 D 1*

## Simple Blessing

Almighty God, who for the salvation of the world
gives to his people many gifts and ministries
to the advancement of his glory,
stir up in you the gifts of his grace,
sustain each one of you in your own ministry;
and the blessing . . .                                       *20 E 1*

## Solemn Blessing

God who has called you is faithful.

The Father, whose glory fills the heavens,
cleanse you by his holiness
and send you to proclaim his word.   **Amen.**

Christ, who has ascended to the heights,
pour upon you the riches of his grace.   **Amen.**

The Holy Spirit, the Comforter,
equip you and strengthen you in your ministry.   **Amen.**

And the blessing . . .                                       *20 F 1*

## THE EUCHARIST

### *Introduction to the Peace*

1   God has reconciled us to himself through Christ
    and given us the ministry of reconciliation.                  *20 G 1*

2   We are all one in Christ Jesus.
    We belong to him through faith,
    heirs of the promise of the Spirit of peace.                  *20 G 2*


### *Eucharistic Preface*

1   And now we give you thanks
    because by your Spirit
    you anointed your only Son to be servant of all
    and ordained that he should enter into his kingdom
         through suffering.
    In your wisdom and love you call your Church
    to serve the world,
    to share in Christ's suffering
    and to reveal his glory.
    Therefore . . .                                               *20 H 1*

2   And now we give you thanks
    because within the royal priesthood of your Church
    you ordain ministers to proclaim the word of God,
    to care for your people
    and to celebrate the sacraments of the new covenant.
    Therefore . . .                                               *20 H 2*

3   And now we give you thanks
    because Christ came not to be served,
    but to serve,
    and to give his life as a ransom for many.
    He calls his faithful servants
    to lead your holy people in love,
    nourishing them by your word and sacraments.
    Therefore . . .                                               *20 H 3*

# Words at the Breaking of Bread

We break this bread
to share in the body of Christ.
**Though we are many we are one body,**
**because we all share in one bread.**

*20 J 1*

# Invitation to Communion

The gifts of God for the people of God.
**Jesus Christ is holy,**
**Jesus Christ is Lord,**
**to the glory of God the Father.**

*20 K 1*

# Prayers after Communion

1   God of power,
    may the boldness of your Spirit transform us,
    may the gentleness of your Spirit lead us,
    may the gifts of your Spirit equip us
    to serve and worship you
    now and always.   **Amen.**

*20 L 1*

2   Eternal Giver of love and life,
    your Son Jesus Christ has sent us into all the world
    to preach the gospel of his kingdom.
    Confirm us in this mission,
    and help us to live the good news we proclaim,
    through Jesus Christ our Lord.   **Amen.**

*20 L 2*

3   Lord of the harvest,
    you have fed your people
    with the holy bread of life.
    We pray you, by your grace,
    raise up among us faithful labourers
    to sow your word and reap the harvest of souls;
    through Jesus Christ our Lord.   **Amen.**

*20 L 3*

4    O God,
      you make your ministers winds
        and your ministers flames of fire;
      stir up and strengthen the sacred gift of orders
      in all stewards of your mysteries,
      that they may gather out of your kingdom
        everything that prevents its growth,
      and may kindle in the hearts of all
        that fire which you came to send on earth;
      to the glory of your name.   **Amen.**        *20 L 4*

## DAILY PRAYER

## *Light Prayer*

Blessed are you, Sovereign God of all,
to you be glory and praise for ever!
From the rising of the sun to its setting
your glory is proclaimed in all the world.
You gave the Christ as a light to the nations,
and through the anointing of his Spirit
you established us as a royal priesthood.
As you call us into his marvellous light,
may our lives bear witness to your truth
and our lips never cease to proclaim your praise,
Father, Son and Holy Spirit.
**Blessed be God for ever!**        *20 M 1*

## *Canticle*

### A SONG OF HOPE

[Response   **I will greatly rejoice in the Lord.**]

1    The Spirit of the Lord God is upon me:
      because the Lord has anointed me
        to bring good tidings to the afflicted.

2    The Lord has sent me to bind up the broken-hearted:
to proclaim liberty for the captives,
    and release for those in prison, [R]

3    to comfort all who mourn:
to bestow on them a crown of beauty instead of ashes,

4    the oil of gladness instead of mourning:
a garment of splendour for the heavy heart.  [R]

5    They shall be called trees of righteousness:
planted for the glory of the Lord.

6    Therefore I will greatly rejoice in the Lord:
my soul shall exult in my God,

7    for God has robed me with salvation as a garment:
and clothed me with integrity as a cloak.  [R]

8    For as the earth brings forth its shoots:
and as a garden causes the seeds to spring up,

9    so the Lord God will cause righteousness and praise:
to spring forth before all the nations.  [R]       *20 N 1*

## *Pattern of Readings with Psalms and Canticles*

1    Exodus 19.3–8
    Psalm 15

2    Numbers 11.16–17,24–28 or
    Numbers 27.15–end
    Psalm 99

3    1 Samuel 3.1–10
    Psalm 63.1–8

4    2 Kings 2.9–15
    Psalm 27.1–9

5    Jeremiah 1.4–10
    Psalm 71.1–8

6       Ephesians 4.11–16
            Psalm 68.1–6,18–20
        or
        1 Corinthians 4.1–7
            Psalm 84

Gospel   Matthew 16.24–27 or
            Luke 10.1–9 or
            John 10.11–16                                    *20 P 1*

## *Ending*

Glory to God:
**whose power, working in us,
can do infinitely more
than we ask or imagine.
Glory to God from generation to generation,
in the Church and in Christ Jesus,
for ever and ever.   Amen.**                          *20 Q 1*

# SOURCES

## CHAPTER 1

1 A 1   *Patterns for Worship* [Psalm 51.17]
1 A 2   David Silk *In Penitence and Faith* (Mowbray 1988) [Daniel 9.9]
1 B 1   David Stancliffe for Portsmouth Cathedral [Psalm 51]
1 C 1   Litany from Canadian *Book of Alternative Services*; concluding collect from David Silk *Prayers for Use at the Alternative Services* (Mowbray 1980) (altered)
1 C 2   Trevor Lloyd
1 D 1   *Te Deum*
1 E 1   ASB Rite A
1 E 2   ASB Rite A
1 F 1   Michael Perham for St George's Church Oakdale
1 G 1   ASB Rite A
1 H 1   ASB Rite A
1 H 2   Canadian *Book of Alternative Services* (altered)
1 H 3   *Roman Missal* (altered)
1 J 1   *Patterns for Worship* [1 Cor 11.26]
1 K 1   ASB Rite A
1 L 1   Canadian *Book of Alternative Services* (altered)
1 L 2   Canadian *Book of Alternative Services* (altered)
1 L 3   Canadian *Book of Alternative Services* (altered)
1 M 1   Canadian *Book of Alternative Services*
1 N 1   The Society of St Francis *Daily Office SSF* [Hosea 6.1–6]
1 N 2   The Society of St Francis *Daily Office SSF* [Isaiah 55.6–11]
1 P 1   David Silk
1 P 2   David Silk
1 Q 1   *Catholic Prayers for Church of England People* (Knott 1959)

## CHAPTER 2

2 X 1   Michael Perham
2 A 1   *Patterns for Worship* [Matthew 5.24]
2 A 2   Michael Perham [Isaiah 66.4,13,18]
2 B 1   Michael Perham [Psalm 103.9,13; 131.3]
2 C 1   *Patterns for Worship*
2 C 2   Michael Perham for St George's Church Oakdale
2 D 1   Michael Perham [Psalms 34, 127 & 128]
2 E 1   *Patterns for Worship* [Ephesians 3.15–19]
2 F 1   *Patterns for Worship*
2 G 1   *Patterns for Worship* [Matthew 12.50, Galatians 6.10]
2 H 1   *The Promise of His Glory* (where no source is given)
2 H 2   ASB Rite A
2 L 1   *Patterns for Worship*
2 L 2   Michael Perham
2 M 1   *Celebrating Common Prayer* (Mowbray 1992)
2 N 1   Michael Vasey
2 P 1   David Silk
2 Q 1   Trevor Lloyd [2 Peter 3.18]

## CHAPTER 3

3 A 1   David Silk *In Penitence and Faith* (Mowbray 1988) [1 Peter 2.24]
3 A 2   David Silk *In Penitence and Faith* (Mowbray 1988) [Romans 5.8]
3 B 1   *Roman Missal*
3 C 1   Michael Perham
3 C 2   Trevor Lloyd
3 D 1   Canadian *Book of Alternative Services*
3 E 1   ASB Rite A
3 F 1   *Patterns for Worship* [Galatians 2.20, 2 Cor 5.15]
3 G 1   *Lent, Holy Week, Easter* [Ephesians 2.13]
3 H 1   ASB Rite A
3 H 2   ASB Rite A
3 H 3   *Roman Missal* (altered)

3 H 4   *Roman Missal* (altered)
3 J  1   Canadian *Book of Alternative Services*
3 K  1   ASB Rite A
3 L  1   *Lent, Holy Week, Easter*
3 L  2   *Lent, Holy Week, Easter*
3 L  3   Canadian *Book of Alternative Services* (altered)
3 M 1   Michael Vasey
3 N 1   *Celebrating Common Prayer* (Mowbray 1992) [Lamentations 1 & 3]
3 N 2   *Celebrating Common Prayer* (Mowbray 1992) (altered) [1 Peter 2.21–24]
3 N 3   *Celebrating Common Prayer* (Mowbray 1992) (altered) [Isaiah 63.1–3,7–9]
3 P  1   David Silk
3 P  2   David Silk
3 Q 1   The Society of St Francis *Daily Office SSF*


## CHAPTER 4

4 A 1   David Silk *In Penitence and Faith* (Mowbray 1988) [1 Cor 5.7,8]
4 A 2   David Silk *In Penitence and Faith* (Mowbray 1988) [Romans 6.10]
4 B 1   *Roman Missal* (altered)
4 C 1   Litany from Canadian *Book of Alternative Services* (altered); concluding collect from *Lent, Holy Week, Easter*
4 C 2   *Patterns for Worship*
4 D 1   Canadian *Book of Alternative Services* [1 Peter 1]
4 D 2   *Patterns for Worship* [2 Tim 2.11–13]
4 E 1   ASB Rite A
4 E 2   ASB Rite A
4 E 3   ASB Rite A
4 E 4   *New Zealand Prayer Book* 1989
4 F 1   Michael Perham for St George's Church Oakdale
4 G 1   ASB Rite A
4 H 1   ASB Rite A

4 H 2 ASB Rite A
4 H 3 ASB Rite A
4 H 4 *Roman Missal* (altered)
4 J 1 Canadian *Book of Alternative Services*
4 K 1 ASB Rite A
4 L 1 Canadian *Book of Alternative Services*
4 L 2 David Silk *Prayers for Use at the Alternative Services* (Mowbray 1980)
4 L 3 *New Zealand Prayer Book* 1989
4 L 4 *Lent, Holy Week, Easter*
4 M 1 Michael Vasey
4 N 1 *New Zealand Prayer Book* 1989 [Exodus 15]
4 N 2 *Celebrating Common Prayer* (Mowbray 1992) (altered)
4 P 1 David Silk
4 P 2 David Silk
4 Q 1 *Lent, Holy Week, Easter*


## CHAPTER 5

5 A 1 ASB Rite B
5 A 2 *Patterns for Worship* [Hebrew 4.15,16]
5 B 1 *Roman Missal* (altered)
5 C 1 Michael Perham
5 D 1 Michael Perham [Ephesians 1.20,22, Colossians 3.1,3,4]
5 E 1 ASB Rite A
5 E 2 *An Australian Prayer Book* 1978
5 F 1 Michael Perham
5 G 1 [John 14.1,27]
5 H 1 ASB Rite A
5 H 2 Book of Common Prayer (altered)
5 H 3 Michael Perham from *Te Deum*
5 H 4 *Patterns for Worship* [Col 1.15–20, Hebrews 1.3, Rev 1.14–18]
5 J 1 Canadian *Book of Alternative Services*
5 K 1 *The Promise of His Glory*
5 K 2 ASB Rite A
5 L 1 Charles MacDonnell *After Communion* (Mowbray 1985)

5 L 2 Canadian *Book of Alternative Services*
5 M 1 Michael Vasey
5 N 1 The Society of St Francis *Daily Office SSF* [Colossians 1.13–20]
5 N 2 The Society of St Francis *Daily Office SSF* [Ephesians 1.3–10]
5 P 1 David Silk
5 P 2 David Silk
5 Q 1 ASB [Ephesians 3.20–21]


## CHAPTER 6

6 A 1 *Patterns for Worship* [John 16.18]
6 A 2 David Silk *In Penitence and Faith* (Mowbray 1988)
6 B 1 David Stancliffe for Portsmouth Cathedral
6 C 1 Kenneth Stevenson for Holy Trinity Church Guildford (altered)
6 D 1 Canadian *Book of Alternative Services* (altered)
6 D 2 Michael Perham for St George's Church Oakdale
6 E 1 ASB Rite A
6 E 2 ASB Rite A
6 F 1 Michael Perham for St George's Church Oakdale
6 G 1 ASB Rite A
6 H 1 ASB Rite A
6 H 2 Canadian *Book of Alternative Services* (altered)
6 H 3 ASB Rite B (altered)
6 J 1 Canadian *Book of Alternative Services*
6 K 1 ASB Rite A
6 L 1 Canadian *Book of Alternative Services* (altered)
6 L 2 *New Zealand Prayer Book* 1989
6 M 1 Michael Vasey
6 N 1 *Celebrating Common Prayer* (Mowbray 1992) [Judith 16.13–16]
6 N 2 *Celebrating Common Prayer* (Mowbray 1992) [Ezekiel 36.24–28]
6 P 1 David Silk
6 P 2 David Silk

6 Q 1   David Silk *Prayers for Use at the Alternative Services* (Mowbray 1980)


## CHAPTER 7

7 A 1   Trevor Lloyd [Isaiah 6.5,7]
7 A 2   John Townend [Matthew 23.37]
7 B 1   Michael Perham
7 B 2   Michael Perham for St George's Church Oakdale [Isaiah 6.3,5,7]
7 B 3   John Townend [Matthew 23.37]
7 C 1   Trevor Lloyd (extended from Edward Cowper's hymn of 1805)
7 D 1   [Revelation 4.11; 5.9,10,13]
7 E 1   ASB Rite A
7 F 1   Michael Perham (based on a prayer of Bishop Thomas Ken)
7 F 2   *Patterns for Worship* [Numbers 6.24–25]
7 G 1   *Patterns for Worship*
7 H 1   ASB Rite A
7 H 2   Michael Perham (adapted from *Te Deum*)
7 J 1   Canadian *Book of Alternative Services*
7 K 1   ASB Rite A
7 L 1   Janet Morley *All Desires Known* (MOW 1988)
7 L 2   Liturgy of Malabar
7 M 1   *Praise God in Song* reproduced in the Canadian *Book of Alternative Services*
7 N 1   *New Zealand Prayer Book* 1989 [1 John 4.7,8,16,18–21]
7 N 2   Michael Vasey
7 P 1   David Silk
7 Q 1   Bishop Thomas Ken (altered)


## CHAPTER 8

8 A 1   Michael Perham [1 John 3.2–3]
8 B 1   Michael Perham [Psalm 36.5,6,9]
8 C 1   Michael Perham (based on the Transfiguration lections)

8 D 1 Michael Perham [Isaiah 60.1–2 & 1 Tim 1.10]
8 E 1 Michael Perham
8 F 1 Michael Perham (adapted from Charles Wesley's hymn)
8 G 1 Michael Perham [Philippians 3.21]
8 H 1 ASB Rite A
8 H 2 *Roman Missal* (altered)
8 J 1 Canadian *Book of Alternative Services*
8 K 1 ASB Rite A
8 L 1 Canadian *Book of Alternative Services*
8 L 2 Charles MacDonnell *After Communion* (Mowbray 1985)
8 M 1 Michael Vasey
8 P 1 David Silk
8 Q 1 ASB [Ephesians 3.20–21]

# CHAPTER 9

9 A 1 Michael Perham [Hebrews 12.22–24]
9 B 1 Michael Perham for St George's Church Oakdale [Isaiah 6]
9 C 1 Michael Perham
9 D 1 Michael Perham [Psalms 91 & 103]
9 E 1 Michael Perham
9 F 1 *Patterns for Worship* (altered)
9 G 1 Michael Perham [Luke 2.14]
9 H 1 ASB Rite A
9 H 2 *Roman Missal* (altered)
9 J 1 Michael Perham for St George's Church Oakdale [Psalm 78.23,24]
9 K 1 *The Promise of His Glory* [Revelation 19.9]
9 L 1 David Silk *Prayers for Use at the Alternative Services* (Mowbray 1980) (altered)
9 L 2 Canadian *Book of Alternative Services*
9 M 1 Michael Vasey
9 P 1 David Silk
9 Q 1 Bishop Thomas Ken (altered)

CHAPTER 10

10 A 1 Trevor Lloyd [1 Cor 6.19–20]
10 B 1 Michael Perham [Psalms 69.9,84.10,121.8]
10 C 1 Canadian *Book of Alternative Services* (altered) .
10 D 1 Michael Perham [Genesis 28.12,17; John 1.50–51; 1 Cor 3.16]
10 E 1 Michael Perham
10 F 1 *Patterns for Worship* (altered)
10 G 1 Traditional text for Blessing of a House
10 H 1 ASB Rite A
10 H 2 ASB Rite B (altered)
10 H 3 *Roman Missal* (altered)
10 J 1 ASB Rite A
10 K 1 ASB Rite A
10 L 1 John Donne
10 L 2 *Roman Missal*
10 L 3 William Temple
10 M 1 Michael Vasey
10 N 1 The Society of St Francis *Daily Office SSF* [Revelation 21.1–5a]
10 P 1 David Silk
10 Q 1 Old Scottish Prayer

CHAPTER 11

11 A 1 Michael Perham [Isaiah 66.4,13,18]
11 B 1 *Roman Missal*
11 C 1 Michael Perham for St George's Church Oakdale; concluding collect from David Silk *Prayers for Use at the Alternative Services* (Mowbray 1980)
11 D 1 Michael Perham [Luke 1.41,45,48–49]
11 E 1 ASB Rite A
11 F 1 *The Promise of His Glory*
11 G 1 *The Promise of His Glory* [Isaiah 9.6]
11 H 1 ASB Rite A
11 H 2 ASB Rite A
11 H 3 Michael Perham (adapted from *Te Deum*)

11 J   1   Canadian *Book of Alternative Services*
11 K   1   *The Promise of His Glory* [Rev 19.9]
11 L   1   Canadian *Book of Alternative Services*
11 L   2   Charles MacDonnell *After Communion* (Mowbray 1985)
11 M   1   *The Promise of His Glory*
11 N   1   *New Zealand Prayer Book* 1989 [1 Samuel 2.1–4,7,8]
11 N   2   The Society of St Francis *Daily Office SSF* [Isaiah
           61.10–11; 62.1–3]
11 N   3   David Silk [Judith 13.18–20; 15.9–10]
11 P   1   David Silk
11 P   2   David Silk
11 Q   1   Michael Perham


CHAPTER   12

12 A   1   David Silk *In Penitence and Faith* (Mowbray 1988)
           [Hebrews 12.1]
12 A   2   David Silk
12 B   1   David Silk
12 B   2   David Silk
12 C   1   Michael Perham; concluding collect ASB
12 C   2   Trevor Lloyd
12 D   1   Canadian *Book of Alternative Services*
12 E   1   ASB Rite A
12 E   2   *Patterns for Worship* (altered)
12 F   1   *Patterns for Worship* (altered) [Eph 1.17–18; Col 1.12; Eph
           2.14]
12 G   1   ASB Rite A
12 H   1   ASB Rite A
12 H   2   *The Promise of His Glory*
12 H   3   *Roman Missal* (altered)
12 J   1   Canadian *Book of Alternative Services*
12 J   2   Canadian *Book of Alternative Services*
12 K   1   *The Promise of His Glory*
12 K   2   ASB Rite A
12 L   1   Canadian *Book of Alternative Services*
12 L   2   *The Promise of His Glory*

12 L  3   Charles McDonnell *After Communion* (Mowbray 1985)
12 M  1   *The Promise of His Glory*
12 M  2   *The Promise of His Glory*
12 N  1   The Society of St Francis *The Daily Office SSF* [Rev 7.9–10,14–17]
12 P  1   David Silk
12 P  2   David Silk
12 Q  1   Mozarabic Sacramentary in *The Promise of His Glory*


CHAPTER  13

13 A  1   *The Promise of His Glory*
13 A  2   David Silk
13 B  1   David Silk
13 B  2   David Silk
13 B  3   David Silk
13 C  1   Michael Perham
13 C  2   *The Promise of His Glory*
13 D  1   Canadian *Book of Alternative Services*
13 E  1   ASB Rite A
13 E  2   ASB Rite A
13 E  3   *New Zealand Prayer Book* 1989
13 F  1   *The Promise of His Glory*
13 G  1   *The Promise of His Glory* [1 Thess 5.23]
13 G  2   *Lent, Holy Week, Easter*
13 H  1   ASB Rite A
13 H  2   ASB Rite A
13 H  3   *Patterns for Worship*
13 H  4   ASB Rite A
13 H  5   Canadian *Book of Alternative Services* (altered)
13 J  1   Canadian *Book of Alternative Services*
13 J  2   Canadian *Book of Alternative Services*
13 K  1   *The Promise of His Glory*
13 L  1   *Patterns for Worship*
13 L  2   David Silk *Prayers for Use at the Alternative Services* (Mowbray 1980) (altered)

13 L  3   Gothic Missal in David Silk *Prayers for Use at the Alternative Services* (Mowbray 1980) (altered)
13 L  4   Canadian *Book of Alternative Services*
13 L  5   Canadian *Book of Alternative Services*
13 L  6   Canadian *Book of Alternative Services*
13 M 1   *Celebrating Common Prayer* (Mowbray 1992)
13 M 2   Michael Vasey
13 N  1   *Patterns for Worship* [Wisdom 10.15–19,20b–21]
13 N  2   *The Promise of His Glory* [Wisdom 14.20a,21,27; 15.1–6]
13 N  3   *Patterns for Worship* [Ecclus 51.13–18a,20b–22]
13 N  4   *The Promise of His Glory* [Wisdom 3.1–8]
13 P  1   David Silk
13 P  2   David Silk
13 P  3   David Silk
13 Q  1   *Patterns for Worship*

## CHAPTER 14

14 A  1   *Patterns for Worship* [Romans 8.22; Genesis 3.18]
14 B  1   David Stancliffe for Portsmouth Cathedral
14 C  1   Michael Perham for St George's Church Oakdale [John 4.35; Genesis 1.26–28; John 16.13; Galatians 5.22; Deuteronomy 8.7–8; 1 Cor 15.23; Rev 14.15, 19.9]
14 D  1   Canadian *Book of Alternative Services*
14 E  1   *Sarum Missal*
14 G  1   *Patterns for Worship* [James 3.18]
14 G  2   Galatians 5.22,25
14 H  1   *Roman Missal* (altered)
14 J  1   *The Didache* in *Patterns for Worship*
14 K  1   *The Promise of His Glory*
14 L  1   *New Zealand Prayer Book* 1989 (altered)
14 L  2   Charles MacDonnell *After Communion* (Mowbray 1985)
14 M 1   *Celebrating Common Prayer* (Mowbray 1992)
14 N  1   Saint Francis in The Society of St Francis *Daily Office Book SSF*
14 P  1   David Silk

14 P   2   David Silk
14 Q   1   Trevor Lloyd


## CHAPTER 15

15 A   1   Order for Remembrance Sunday in *The Promise of His Glory*
15 B   1   Trevor Lloyd for Holy Trinity Church Wealdstone
15 B   2   *The Promise of His Glory*
15 C   1   *The Promise of His Glory*
15 C   2   Trevor Lloyd (based on the Letter of James)
15 D   1   Canadian *Book of Alternative Services*
15 E   1   *Patterns for Worship* [2 Thess 3.16]
15 E   2   *The Promise of His Glory*
15 F   1   *Patterns for Worship* (altered) [Acts 17.26; Rev 5.9]
15 G   1   *Patterns for Worship* [Eph 2.14–15]
15 G   2   *Patterns for Worship* [Matthew 5.9]
15 H   1   *The Promise of His Glory*
15 H   2   *The Promise of His Glory*
15 H   3   Trevor Lloyd
15 K   1   ASB Rite A
15 L   1   Presbyterian Church USA *Daily Prayer: The Worship of God*
15 L   2   *New Zealand Prayer Book* 1989 (altered)
15 L   3   *The Promise of His Glory*
15 L   4   Canadian *Book of Alternative Services*
15 M   1   Michael Vasey
15 N   1   *The Promise of His Glory* [Matthew 5.3–12]
15 N   2   *The Promise of His Glory* [Isaiah 2.3–5]
15 P   1   David Silk
15 P   2   David Silk
15 Q   1   Traditional


## CHAPTER 16

16 A   1   Titus 2.11
16 A   2   David Silk *In Penitence and Faith* (Mowbray 1988) [Romans 5.8]

16 B  1  *Roman Missal*
16 B  2  *Roman Missal*
16 C  1  Michael Perry *Church Family Worship* (Hodder 1986)
16 C  2  *Patterns for Worship*
16 D  1  *Patterns for Worship* [Ezekiel 47; Rev 22]
16 E  1  *New Zealand Prayer Book* 1989
16 E  2  *The Promise of His Glory*
16 F  1  *Patterns for Worship* [Numbers 6.24–25]
16 G  1  *The Promise of His Glory* [John 14.27]
16 G  2  *Patterns for Worship*
16 H  1  ASB Rite A (altered)
16 H  2  Adapted from a text in *The Promise of His Glory*
16 J  1  Canadian *Book of Alternative Services* [John 6.48,51; Psalm 34.8]
16 K  1  ASB Rite A
16 L  1  Canadian *Book of Alternative Services*
16 L  2  *New Zealand Prayer Book* 1989 (altered)
16 L  3  Canadian *Book of Alternative Services* (altered)
16 L  4  Charles MacDonnell *After Communion* (Mowbray 1985)
16 M  1  *Celebrating Common Prayer* (Mowbray 1992)
16 N  1  *Patterns for Worship* [Isaiah 35.2–6,10]
16 P  1  David Silk
16 P  2  David Silk
16 Q  1  Trevor Lloyd *Liturgy and Death* (Grove 1974)

## CHAPTER 17

17 A  1  Michael Perham [Titus 3.5]
17 B  1  David Stancliffe for Portsmouth Cathedral
17 C  1  ASB Litany; the concluding collect from *The Promise of His Glory*
17 C  2  Michael Perham: the concluding collect ASB
17 D  1  *Patterns for Worship* [Romans 6]
17 D  2  Derived from the Byzantine rite and in *The Promise of His Glory*
17 E  1  ASB Rite A

17 E 2 David Stancliffe for Portsmouth Cathedral
17 F 1 Southwark Diocese
17 G 1 ASB Rite A
17 G 2 Portsmouth Cathedral
17 H 1 ASB Rite A
17 H 2 ASB Rite A
17 H 3 *Roman Missal* (altered)
17 H 4 Canadian *Book of Alternative Services* (altered)
17 J 1 Canadian *Book of Alternative Services*
17 K 1 ASB Rite A
17 L 1 Canadian *Book of Alternative Services* (altered)
17 L 2 *New Zealand Prayer Book* 1989 (altered)
17 L 3 David Silk *Prayers for Use at the Alternative Services* (Mowbray 1980)
17 L 4 Charles MacDonnell *After Communion* (Mowbray 1985)
17 M 1 Michael Vasey
17 N 1 *Patterns for Worship* [Isaiah 12.2–6]
17 N 2 *Celebrating Common Prayer* (Mowbray 1992) [Revelation 21 & 22]
17 P 1 David Silk
17 Q 1 Michael Perham

CHAPTER 18

18 A 1 *Patterns for Worship* [Hebrews 4.12]
18 B 1 Portsmouth Cathedral
18 B 2 *The Promise of His Glory*
18 C 1 *Patterns for Worship*
18 D 1 Michael Perham [Isaiah 55.3,8; John 5.39; Romans 15.4]
18 E 1 *Patterns for Worship*
18 G 1 *Patterns for Worship* [1 Samuel 12.22]
18 H 1 *Patterns for Worship* (altered)
18 H 2 ASB Rite A
18 J 1 Michael Perham [Ps 119.103; John 6.48; Ps 34.8]
18 K 1 ASB Rite A
18 L 1 David Silk *Prayers for Use at the Alternative Services* (Mowbray 1980)

18 L 2 Canadian *Book of Alternative Services* (altered)
18 L 3 Westcott House
18 M 1 Bryan Spinks *Christ our Light* (Kevin Mayhew 1990)
18 N 1 *Patterns for Worship* [Isaiah 55.6–11]
18 P 1 David Silk
18 P 2 David Silk
18 Q 1 *Patterns for Worship*


CHAPTER 19

19 A 1 Book of Common Prayer (altered)
19 B 1 David Stancliffe for Portsmouth Cathedral
19 B 2 *Roman Missal*
19 C 1 Michael Perham
19 D 1 Michael Perham [John 6.33,34,54,63]
19 E 1 ASB Rite A
19 F 1 Michael Perham
19 G 1 ASB Rite B
19 G 2 *The Promise of His Glory*
19 H 1 ASB Rite A
19 H 2 ASB Rite B (altered)
19 H 3 *The Promise of His Glory*
19 H 4 *Roman Missal* (altered)
19 J 1 *The Didache* in *Patterns for Worship*
19 K 1 *The Promise of His Glory*
19 L 1 Canadian *Book of Alternative Services*
19 L 2 *The Promise of His Glory*
19 L 3 David Silk *Prayers for Use at the Alternative Services* (Mowbray 1980)
19 L 4 Charles MacDonnell *After Communion* (Mowbray 1985)
19 N 1 *Patterns for Worship* (altered) (Wisdom 16.20–21,26]
19 P 1 David Silk
19 P 2 David Silk
19 Q 1 Michael Perham [Proverbs 9.2,5,6; Ps 43.1]

# CHAPTER 20

20 A 1  *The Promise of His Glory* (altered)
20 B 1  Trevor Lloyd
20 B 2  Trevor Lloyd
20 C 1  Michael Perry *Church Family Worship* (Hodder 1986) (altered)
20 D 1  *Patterns for Worship* [1 Cor 12.4–6; Eph 4.4–13]
20 E 1  ASB (altered)
20 F 1  Michael Perham
20 G 1  *Patterns for Worship* [2 Cor 5.18]
20 G 2  *Patterns for Worship* [Galatians 3.28]
20 H 1  ASB Rite A
20 H 2  ASB Rite A
20 H 3  Canadian *Book of Alternative Services* (altered)
20 J 1  ASB
20 K 1  ASB Rite A
20 L 1  *New Zealand Prayer Book* 1989 (altered)
20 L 2  *New Zealand Prayer Book* 1989
20 L 3  Charles MacDonnell *After Communion* (Mowbray 1985)
20 L 4  Henry Liddon
20 M 1  *Celebrating Common Prayer* (Mowbray 1992)
20 N 1  *Patterns for Worship* [Isaiah 61.1–3,10,11]
20 P 1  David Silk
20 Q 1  *Patterns for Worship* [Ephesians 3.20–21]